Autism Support Tools
For
Parents and Caregivers

by
Dr. Terita F. Gusby

DR. TERITA F. GUSBY

All rights reserved. No part of this book may be reproduced in any form or by any electronic or mechanical means including information storage and retrieval systems, without permission in writing from the author.

Printed in the United States of America
Blood Drop Inheritance Group
First Printing: March 2025

Copyright © 2024 by Dr. Terita F. Gusby
All rights reserved.
https:www.educationpresciptions.org

Graphic Artist – Danielle Rath

ISBN: 9798313805702

A Starfish Story

A young girl was walking along a beach upon which thousands of starfish had been washed up during a terrible storm. When she came to each starfish, she would pick it up, and throw it back into the ocean. People watched her with amusement.

She had been doing this for some time when a man approached her and said, "Little girl, why are you doing this? Look at this beach! You can't save all these starfish. You can't begin to make a difference!"

The girl seemed crushed, suddenly deflated. But after a few moments, she bent down, picked up another starfish, and hurled it as far as she could into the ocean. Then she looked up at the man and replied, "Well, I made a difference to that one!"

— Adapted from The Star Thrower
by Loren C. Eiseley

GodVine.com

DEDICATION

This book is dedicated to all the parents, caregivers, teachers, and families who make a difference in the lives of children with autism. It is for people who need daily encouragement, ideas, and support. This book is for you who have not given up, forgotten, or dismissed the fight. You understand the challenge and strength needed to complete the work. This book is a resting spot for you to breathe, regroup and fortify yourself with new tools for your journey. It is to my grandson "EJ" and his parents who have not given up on discovering, learning, and becoming excited with life despite Autism.

Dr. Terita F. Gusby

DR. TERITA F. GUSBY

Meet The Author

Dr. Terita F. Gusby is currently the CEO/ Founder of Education Prescriptions, a virtual education company serving special needs students, grades K12, with an emphasis on students with autism spectrum disorders. She has a doctorate in Curriculum & Instruction and a Master of Science in Urban Education-Diversity, from Kansas State University. She has 2 Bachelor of Science degrees, one in Elementary Education K-8 and one in Special Education K-12 from Culver-Stockton University in the U.S.A.

She has spent over 30 years in Education, and she is presently the Creator of the Autism Academic Learning System which has raised student learning levels, supported parents, and developed self-esteem and self-confidence for learning.

DR. TERITA F. GUSBY

TABLE OF CONTENTS

Forward..8

Contributing Authors..10

Chapter 1 / What We Know About Autism.....................14

Chapter 2/ Early Signs of Autism................................24

Chapter 3/ Understanding Behavior ….........................32

Chapter 4/ Gestures and Body Movements.....................44

Chapter 5 / Indicators of Development..........................54

Chapter 6 / Classroom Stories....................................62

Chapter 7/ Engleman's Syndrome - A Mother's Story..........70

Chapter 8 / Picky Eaters and Good Nutrition....................76

Chapter 9 / Housing and Special Needs........................108

Chapter 10 / Traveling with Autism.............................132

Chapter 11 / Age Transitions....................................147

Chapter 12 / Virtual Learning Help.............................155

Directory of Agencies...195

International Autism Agencies ………………..……….217

References ……………………………………………….237

FORWARD

People often stare at others who are different looking than they are or exhibit behaviors they are not accustomed to. It may be the clothes they wear, the language they speak, their physical movement or even body structure. If it's different, it deserves attention. Many times, people become afraid of what they do not understand. People with special needs, whether physical or mental, inherently come under scrutiny because of their differences.

Autism is rapidly becoming one of the fastest diagnosed categories under special education. In past years it was common to hear terms or categories such as: ADHD or ADD, Emotionally Disturbed, Behavioral Disordered, Deaf, Blind, and Downs Syndrome, and Mentally Handicapped, however, in present day more and more children are being listed under the category of having autism. With these children there comes a list of behaviors and symptoms that tend to be unsettling for people unfamiliar with autism to understand.

Parents who have children with autism have become accustomed to the long stares or movements of people not knowing what to do or how to maneuver around a public physical tantrum or verbal outburst. This book serves as a guide to help parents and caregivers understand how autism affects loved ones and hopefully, they will pass information on to other family members and friends that will allow children with autism to function and feel a part of a world and society, quite different than their own.

It becomes the work of the few - to educate the many - in making the world a safe space for all people to live in no matter the difference….

Dr. Terita Gusby

Contributing Authors

Natalie Pelto

Is an international public speaker & educator with multiple nutrition and lifestyle certifications focused on improving autism outcomes through health & advanced brain development practices and education. She provides resources for mothers, pediatricians and physicians through her "Blue Life Autism Building Brilliant Brains Program".

Natalie is described as the "food is medicine queen" and best picky eating strategist by the members of her community. She lives in Northern Canada, in the Muskokas (God's country) makes different treatment options for autism available in lifestyle and improved outcomes so kids with autism can offer their unique gifts to the world.

Danielle Terrell

Danielle Terrell gravitated to the human service field 7 years ago. Danielle has worked in community services, public education, residential services, and support coordination. She worked as a Registered Behavior Technician for several years providing ABA services to young children and adolescents. She applied this practice to individual programming for adults living in an assisted living facility. She has lived in multiple states in the United States along the East Coast, which has given her perspective as to the varying degrees of services provided from state to state.

She earned a Master of Science in Developmental Disabilities from Nova Southeastern University in 2021. Her graduate studies put a heavy emphasis on staffing, housing, and healthcare issues. Outside of her professional titles, she is a volunteer with "Autism on the Seas," and a volunteer and affiliate of the" Global Autism Project."

Dr. Fida Yousef Ahmed Diab

Dr. Fida resides and works in the United Arab Emirates. She is the Head of the Support Team for People of Determination Center. She holds prestigious memberships in the following organizations: Emirates Autism Society; Hamma Association for Mothers of People of Determination; Emirates Rare Society; Breastfeeding Association; Sand First Aid; Friends of Senior Citizens Association: Organizing Committee of the Regional Conference, Earn People of Determination 2022; Organizing Committee of the

DR. TERITA F. GUSBY

Rare Diseases Conference 2022; Board of Trustees of Al-Itqan School; Ajman Societies Association; Representative of the Help and Bob Center in the Middle East and North Africa, and winner of the Sharjah Award for Voluntary Work. She is an international computer trainer with 25 years of experience in technology and as a media film director. She holds an honorary doctorate from the Canadian International Academy and a certificate from the International Institute for Protocol and Etiquette.

She is the middle east consultant in the continuing education sector at the British University in Fujairah. She has held many conferences and educational workshops in the Middle East as well as internationally. Dr. Fida has accrued training hours in disability and self-development. She is an international trainer accredited by the European Board. She is the mother of a child suffering from a rare syndrome called Engelman Syndrome. She is a sixteen-year-old who has shown similar behaviors and signs like Autism.

DR. TERITA F. GUSBY

Chapter 1

What We Know About Autism

According to the Child Mind Institute Family Resource Center, autism spectrum disorder (ASD) is a neurodevelopmental disorder, which means that it impacts how a child develops. Autism begins in utero, although children with ASD might not be diagnosed until they are in preschool – or even school-aged (or older), when signs of the disorder become more apparent. Children with ASD have a combination of two kinds of behaviors: deficits in communication and social skills, and the presence of restricted behaviors. It's called a spectrum because individuals with the disorder may have a wide range of symptoms, cognitive abilities, language skills and behaviors.

The Children's Health Act of 2000 authorized the Centers for Disease Control and Prevention (CDC) to create the Autism and Developmental Disabilities Monitoring (ADDM) Network to track the number and characteristics of children with autism spectrum disorder (ASD)* and other developmental disabilities in diverse communities throughout the United States. The Center of Disease Control reports that about 1 in 36 children in the United States is diagnosed with an autism spectrum disorder.

- 2.8% of 8- year-old children have been diagnosed with ASD.
- Boys are four times more likely to be diagnosed with autism than girls.
- The previous estimate from 2020 found a prevalence of 1 in 44 (2.3%).

Sensory Processing Concerns

Rutgers researchers say that advances in diagnostic capabilities, greater understanding and awareness of ASD, and genetic environmental factors may be contributing to the increase in autism rates. A clinical psychologist says that the rising rates can be attributed to multiple factors including increased access to care, awareness, and screening. Children with autism want to behave appropriately and follow the rules but have a difficult time applying their memory of rules to real life situations especially when they are anxious, impulsive, or confused. Children with autism have trouble understanding how to apply to school and the social rules they seem to break. In some cases, these students may correct others who break the rules, the ones that they understand and are simple in nature.

Because of this variability in understanding rules and actual performance of appropriate behaviors - educators, family and peers often are unsure about the area of discipline as it applies to students with autism. How do you develop appropriate behavior for your child?

In some people, the brain has trouble organizing and responding to information from the senses. Certain sounds, sights, smells, textures, and tastes can create a feeling of "sensory overload." Bright or flickering lights, loud noises, certain textures of food, and scratchy clothing are just some of the triggers that can make kids feel overwhelmed and upset. What are sensory processing issues?

The term refers to trouble managing information that comes in through the senses. These issues, sometimes called sensory processing disorder or sensory integration disorder, can have a big impact on learning and on everyday life.

Autistic kids often express a strong preference for foods that feel a certain way in their mouths. Some prefer soft or creamy foods like yogurt, soup or ice cream; others need the stimulation that crunchy foods like Cheetos or — if a parent is lucky, carrots can provide it. In either case, that can put significant limitations on the different foods' kids are willing to eat.

Underdeveloped oral motor musculature: Kids who eat almost exclusively soft foods may lack the muscle development that it takes to chew foods like steak or hamburger. Parents who don't know this is the cause of their child's distress will respond by allowing them to forget the foods that would strengthen those muscles, so it becomes a vicious cycle.

Time and behavior at the table: Lots of parents experience the frustration of trying to get their children to sit at the table long enough to finish a meal. But with autistic kids the challenge can be magnified, and there is also the issue of safety. Unsafe behaviors might include throwing utensils or repeatedly getting up and running from the table.

For children and families who are struggling with an autistic child's rigid eating habits, consulting a feeding specialist could be a child psychologist, speech-language pathologist or occupational therapist — can be helpful.

Communication

Signs of a deficit in communication and social skills may include, but are not limited to, a combination of the following:

In Younger Children Under 3-

- Failure to respond to their name.
- Disinterest in giving, sharing or showing objects of interest.
- Aversions to affection
- Preference to solitary play

In Older Children-

- Difficulty in a reciprocal or back-and-forth conversation.
- Lack of eye contact
- Difficulty using and reading body language in others.
- Difficulty recognizing others' emotions, responding appropriately to different social situations, and understanding social relationships.
- Aversions to displays of affection.
- Preference to solitary play

Children with restricted or repetitive behaviors perform repetitive actions and rituals and can become fixated on minute details to the point of distraction. In addition, they may:

- Become upset by minor changes in a daily routine.
- Line, sort, or organize toys or objects instead of playing with them.
- Show a consuming interest in a specific topic or object.

- Have unusual sensory sensitivities.

To meet the criteria for ASD, a child's symptoms in these two areas must be present in early childhood, though they may not become fully clear until later, when social demands exceed limited capabilities. Alternatively, they may be clear early on and then masked later by learned behaviors. These symptoms must also cause clinically significant impairment in social, occupational, academic, or other important areas of functioning. In addition to the two required criteria to meet the diagnosis, children with autism spectrum disorder often have sensory issues and varying cognitive and verbal abilities.

Parents, grandparents, early childhood education providers, and other caregivers can participate in developmental monitoring. The Centre for Disease Control (2023) issued out a **Learn the Signs, Act Early** Program that has developed free materials, including **CDC's Milestone Tracker** app, to help parents and providers work together to monitor your child's development and know when there might be a concern and if more screening is needed. You can use a brief checklist of milestones to see how your child is developing. If you notice that your child is not meeting milestones, talk with your doctor or nurse about your concerns and ask about developmental screening. Learn more about CDC **Milestone Tracker** app, milestone checklists, and other parent materials at *https://www.cdc.gov/index.htm*.

When you take your child to a well visit, your doctor or nurse will also do developmental monitoring. The doctor or nurse might ask you questions about your child's development or will talk and play with your child to see if they are developing and meeting milestones.

Your doctor or nurse may also ask about your child's family history. Be sure to let your doctor or nurse know about any conditions that your child's family members have, including ASD, learning disorders, intellectual disability, or attention deficit/hyperactivity disorder (ADHD).

A brief test using a screening tool does not provide a diagnosis, but it can indicate whether a child is on the right development track or if a specialist should take a closer look. If the screening tool identifies an area of concern, a formal developmental evaluation may be needed. This formal evaluation is a more in-depth look at a child's development and is usually done by a, child psychologist, speech-language pathologist, occupational therapist, or other specialist.

The specialist may observe and then give the child a structured test, ask the parents or caregivers questions, or ask them to fill out questionnaires. The results of this formal evaluation highlight your child's strengths and challenges and can inform you whether they meet criteria for a developmental diagnosis. A diagnosis of ASD now includes several conditions that used to be diagnosed separately; autistic disorder, pervasive developmental disorder not otherwise specified (PDD-NOS), and Asperger syndrome. Your doctor or other healthcare provider can help you understand and navigate the diagnostic process.

The results of a formal developmental evaluation can also inform whether your child needs early intervention services. In some cases, the specialist might <u>recommend genetic counseling and testing for your child</u>. All young children need both developmental monitoring and developmental screening. The best person to track your child's development is you! Share your child's milestone checklist and any related information from your child's teachers or other providers with the doctor at every well-child visit. What if your child is not reaching milestones as expected? You know your child best. If you are concerned about your child's development, talk with your child's doctor about your concerns and ask about developmental screening. For more information, go to <u>www.cdc.gov/</u> If you are concerned.......... Don't wait! Acting early can make a real difference.

Early identification remains a major focus of CDC's ADDM Network, as it is one of the most important tools communities have in helping to make a difference in the lives of children with ASD. The earlier that children are identified with ASD, the earlier they can access services and support.

DR. TERITA F. GUSBY

Chapter 2

<u>Early Signs of Autism</u>

Identifying Autism Spectrum Disorder (ASD) at the earliest possible age is of the utmost importance — early treatment can be very beneficial to the child and their family. Abnormalities in how babies act socially, as well as how they pay attention to and interact with their non-social environment, could be early warning signs. A delay in speech alone generally does not signify autism, but in combination with other warning signs, could suggest that a toddler is at risk.

When a child at-risk for autism there may appear problems when he speaks, and the voice might not vary in pitch, tone, or volume. The vocalizations of children who are not yet speaking might sound more like non-word sounds (e.g., whining, fussing, growling) than like parts of words. Typically, <u>children will begin to</u>

speak between 12 and 18 months, advancing from cooing and singular words to a broader range of sounds by 18 to 24 months. For children with autism, verbal communication usually begins around 36 months (three years old). While this is the most common time, children with autism might start speaking as late as five years old. It's important to note that around 25-30% of children with ASD say fewer than 30 words or may not speak at all. According the American Paediatric Association the following behaviours and explanations are beneficial when considering a child having developmental learning concerns in identifying autism:

Delay in or lack of joint attention

According to the American Academy of Paediatrics, one of the most important developmental differences between children on the autism spectrum and children without ASD is a delay in or lack of **joint attention**. In fact, delays in joint attention skills are found in most children with autism spectrum disorder.

What is joint attention?

Joint attention is looking back and forth between an object, event, or another person and connecting with that person. It is a building block for later social and communication skills. Engaging in many back-and-forth social interactions, such as exchanging a lot of emotional expressions, sounds and other gestures, are considered **social interactions**.

Stages of Joint Attention in Babies & Toddlers

There are several stages of joint attention. Children on the autism spectrum usually show delayed or absent social communication skills at every stage. For example, below are the ages when babies and toddlers typically use and understand gestures at the following times, compared with young children on the autism spectrum:

Using & understanding gestures such as pointing

- **By 12 months of age**

- o **Most children** can immediately look in the direction of an object a parent is pointing at. They will then look back at the parent and mimic the parent's expression, usually a smile.

- o **Children on the autism spectrum may appear to ignore their parents. This can cause parents to worry about their child's <u>hearing</u>.**

- **By 15 months of age**

  - o **Most children** can point to out-of-reach objects that they want.

  - o **A child on the autism spectrum** may instead take a parent's hand and lead the parent to the object without making much, if any, eye contact. Sometimes the child may even place the parent's hand onto the object itself.

- **By 18 months of age**

Most children point at objects they find interesting. Children will look back and forth between an object and a parent to make sure the parent is tuned in to what they are looking at. **At this age a child should be able to point to communicate or indicate that they want something. It could be food, a toy or even to get a person's attention.** Children on the autism disorder spectrum will often point to an object because they want a parent to get it for them, not because they want the parent to enjoy looking at the object with them.

Language delays & differences with ASD

Almost all children on the autism disorder spectrum show delays in nonverbal communication and spoken language. For example, you may notice differences such as:

The use of labels

A child on the autism spectrum may have words they use to label things, for example, but not to ask for things. They may use words for objects before using words for people or family members.

Echoing & repeating

Most young children go through a phase when they repeat what they hear. Children on the the autism spectrum may repeat what they hear for a longer period. They also may repeat dialogue from movies or conversations with the tone of voice they heard them in. This is called **parroting** or **echoing**. Some children later diagnosed with the autism spectrum will seem to have met language milestones during the toddler years. However, their use of language may be unusual. For example, they may talk more like an adult than a toddler.

Regression in developmental milestones & skills

About 25% of children later diagnosed with autism spectrum disorder may develop some language that they suddenly or gradually stop using. Typically, this may happen between the ages of 15 and 24 months. They might also become more socially withdrawn. This change is called a regression in skills.

Examples -Understanding language and names of objects –

If you hand your child a cup and tell him to place it on the table and he remains standing with the cup and not moving, you can assume he didn't hear you or doesn't understand the directional language or object identifier in the statement. He may not understand cup / table / or the action, 'put it on the table, "If he takes the cup and places, it somewhere other than the table, he may have a problem with knowing the names of objects (table.)

Being fixated on one object for hours

It is not uncommon for a child to be fixated on an object for a long period of time and ignore everything else that is going on around him. It may be the color, texture, or sound that has gotten his attention. Oftentimes you can use another object to draw his attention away from the previous one. The object can be a body part. A child can become fixated with his hand and the fingers on it. Hands tend to be common body parts that interest children with autism. Because the fingers can move and the hand can when touching the other one, can make a noise (clapping) it becomes an easy one to be drawn to for a long period of time.

Chapter 3

Understanding Behavior

Each child with autism is unique and as the child grows up there will be unique challenges. Teaching appropriate behavior is vital to the child's quality of life. Behavior will be the catalyst for the child to live amicably within the world, however, the uniqueness of each child requires people to accept some behaviors that may seem a bit odd at times. The child may have unique ways to calm down and keep anxiety levels at a minimum. The child may engage in these behaviors without regard to who is around or where they are. This makes the case that teaching appropriate behaviors will make the child not so obviously different from their surroundings.

Stereotypic behavior is one of the main features of autistic individuals, including a wide range of behaviors. There are two common classifications of this behavior: 1) lower-order stereotypic behavior and higher-order stereotypic behavior, and 2) repetitive sensory-motor (RSM) behaviors and repetitive hand mannerisms and insistence on sameness behaviors (Joyce et al., 2020). Autistic children exhibit poor coordination between fine and gross skills (gross skills include big muscles, fine skills involve small muscles) and difficulties in balance, flexibility, and speed (Hassani et al., 2020). Hence, various previous therapies suggested physical activities-based interventions to reduce such types of behaviors and develop coordination skills of autistic children. The need for and acceptance of the behavior should always be acknowledged. Tolerance of differences and acceptance of behaviors that are unique should be fostered.

Strategies

ABA stands for *Applied Behavior Analyses.* It is a set of principles that form the basis for many behavioral treatments. ABA is based on the science of learning and behavior. This science includes general "laws" about how behavior works and how learning takes place. As a parent you become the authority of your child's behavior. You have learned what he reacts to, when he reacts to it and how he reacts to it. You have observed that in certain situations he may become irritable to the point that he has an emotional outburst or reacts favorably to stimulus given.

ABA therapy applies these laws to behavior treatments in a way that helps to increase useful or desired behaviors or to help reduce behaviors that may interfere with learning or behaviors that may be harmful. ABA therapy is used to increase language and communication skills. It is also used to improve attention, focus, social skills, memory, and academics. ABA can be used to help decrease problem behaviors.

"Evidence based" means that ABA has passed scientific tests of its usefulness, quality, and effectiveness. ABA therapy includes many different techniques. When teachers are given the assignment of writing up a behavior program for a child, they are usually asked questions about specific things that happen before the "behavior" starts. They often find that there are patterns that can be followed that a child has gotten used to exhibiting a certain behavior. For instance, if all the children are coloring pictures in class and the teacher says, "Okay let's put away our crayons and get ready for lunch. This announcement for the class could be one that renders a positive response or one rendering a negative one.

The teacher may have to find a different way to get students ready to transition to different activities. The same happens at home. If a parent says, "Okay time to get ready for bed." This could set off an array of negative reactions and then behaviors showing the child's reaction to stopping an activity and beginning a complete shutdown.

All these techniques focus on antecedents (what happens before a behavior occurs) and on consequences (what happens after the behavior). One technique is "positive reinforcement." When a behavior is followed by something that is valued (a reward), that behavior is more likely to be repeated. ABA uses positive reinforcement in a way that can be measured to help bring about meaningful behavior change.

Any ABA therapy plan is made up of some key ingredients that will be necessary as a framework for a more individualized plan. An example of some of these are reinforcement, behavior definitions, prompts, structured teaching moments, natural teaching moments, etc. All these ABA strategies are taken as a general idea and would be specifically molded to fit your child's needs and skill sets. They also are adapted and individualized based on certain behaviors that are being targeted or certain skills that need more development. The following will illustrate more about these specific ideas.

Mental, behavioral, and developmental disorders, such as **anxiety, attention-deficit/hyperactivity disorder or ADHD, and learning problems**, often begin in early childhood and can affect life-long health and well-being. Children with these disorders face challenges at home, at school, and with friends. About 1 in 7 U.S. children aged 2-8 years have a mental, behavioral, and/or developmental disorder.

Previous research has shown that children with mental, behavioral, and developmental disorders and their families face personal, financial, and neighborhood challenges more often than families of children without these disorders. These challenges may make it harder for some parents to give their child the resources they need to thrive. The type of community that families live in, urban versus rural, may increase these challenges. Each child with autism is unique and as the child grows up there will be unique challenges.

Teaching appropriate behavior is vital to the child's quality of life. Behavior will be the catalyst for the child to live amicably within the world. However, the uniqueness of each child requires people to accept some behaviors that may seem a bit odd at times. The child may have unique ways to calm down and keep anxiety levels at a minimum. The child may engage in these behaviors without regard to who is around or where they are. This makes the case that teaching appropriate behaviors will make the child not so obviously different from the surroundings.

Stereotypic behavior is one of the key features of autistic individuals, including a wide range of behaviors. There are two common classifications of this behavior 1) lower-order stereotypic behavior and higher-order stereotypic behavior, and 2) repetitive sensory-motor (RSM) behaviors and repetitive hand mannerisms and insistence on sameness behaviors (Joyce et al., 2017).

Autistic children exhibit poor coordination between fine and gross skills (gross skills include big muscles, fine skills involve small muscles) and difficulties in balance, flexibility, and speed (Hassani et al., 2020). Hence, various previous therapies suggested physical activities-based interventions to reduce such types of behaviors and develop coordination skills of autistic children. The need for and acceptance of the behavior should always be acknowledged.

Tolerance of differences and acceptance of behaviors that are unique should be fostered. A child with autism is often corrected so much so that the world seems like an unfriendly place to be. Channeling behaviors, accounting for special needs, and fostering strengths and interests while building skills and successful experiences are the cornerstone of helping the child grow and learn successfully. There should be an emphasis on cooperation versus competition in all things. In this way, we build a community of learners for all concerned.

Communication With Your Child

Your child communicates in many ways such as:

a. whines/cries

b. reaches toward object.

c. points to object

d. hands over the object.

e. uses gestures or sign language.

f. shows a picture of the object.

g. vocalizes sounds; uses one word or phrase.

Your child also communicates for many reasons.

a. to request

b. to protest

c. to comment

d. to answer questions.

e. to ask questions.

Your child communicates when and where he/she needs or wants to communicate. This can be early in the morning, in the afternoon or after dinner. It can be at home, at the park, or while you are shopping. The best time to teach communication skills is when and where your child needs or wants to communicate.

The three steps to remember to encourage your child to communicate are:

    a. <u>WATCH</u> - to see what your child is interested in and watch for signs that the child is communicating.

    b. <u>WAIT</u> - don't talk or ask questions for a few moments to give your child a chance to initiate communication (at least 5 seconds).

c. <u>FOLLOW YOUR CHILD'S LEAD -</u> talk about and play with the materials that the child is interested in.

<u>Establish and Follow a Routine</u>

All children feel safe when they can follow an established routine, but this is especially important for autistic children. When something is predictable it creates a sense of safety and security, a perceived consistency in structure. Hence a lack of routine can cause anxiety or frustration–<u>which often leads to problem behaviors</u>. This is why it's important to create a schedule that your child can easily stick to. While activities such as appointments or meals can stray from predicted timelines, try to stick to a routine to the best of your ability. You will see results with improved cooperation and emotional health!

Helping a child stick to a schedule can greatly benefit their overall development. To help your autistic child with routine, you can keep transitions predictable, use positive reinforcement and visuals, and above all else, be patient and understanding!

You can also help your child prepare for change! As a parent, you are knowledgeable of most upcoming changes or transitions.

<u>Below are some helpful tips:</u>

- <u>Introduce small changes.</u> By introducing small shifts in routine or expectation, your child can become comfortable with the idea of light change. For instance, you can have your child dressed for the day after breakfast- opposed to their normal routine of dressing before breakfast. Working your way up from small switches can build tolerance.

- <u>Tell a social story</u>. Social stories are a way to narrate specific situations or problems- and how you can overcome them. For example, you could tell a story about going to the mall. You can explain that you'll go to "x, y, z" stores, look for x items, will stop for lunch, and leave at around 2 pm. End your new situation with a positive activity, like going home to watch your child's favorite movie!

- Extra time. Give your child extra time to process new changes and help them get ready for it. By not suddenly launching a new change, your child will feel more comfortable adapting.

- Use a visual schedule. Try as you might, it can be hard to start or end activities right on the dot. Because of this, some autistic children get upset when the schedule isn't going exactly as planned. A visual schedule can depict a general routine, such as a birthday cake (symbolizing a birthday party) following a sandwich (lunchtime), so they know what they're anticipating in their day-to-day schedule through pictures. If your child begins to feel overwhelmed, refer to the schedule, as pictures are a great use of visual support.

Chapter 4

Gestures and Body Movements

Stereotypical behavior is one of the most common characteristics of individuals presenting with autism spectrum disorder (ASD) (Bremer et al., 2016). Stereotypic behavior exhibits a narrower range of interests or activities (Polak et al., 2019). According to the Diagnostic and Statistical Manual of Mental Disorders (DSM-5), stereotypic behavior is a range of purposeless and repetitive motor actions (e.g., hand flapping or hitting) that are commonly predominant and prevalent among neurodevelopmental disorders such as ASD (The American Psychiatric Association [APA], 2013).

These purposeless rituals and monotonous routine actions negatively impact children's daily life and induce major difficulties in learning and adaptation (Patriquin et al., 2017; Ugljevik et al., 2020). Furthermore, individuals presenting stereotypic behavior experience affiliate stigma, social isolation, and public rejecting attitudes and are more likely to be bullied (Lu et al., 2021). Many efforts consequently evoke the various types of treatment and early interventions to reduce by frequency or nature of these meaningless repetitive behaviors among these children (Bremer et al., 2016). In this study, stereotypical behavior is defined as negative monotonous, repetitive actions that children presented with ASD exhibits, such as verbal expressions and physical movements.

What is Stimming?

Stimming can take the form of hand flapping, verbal noises or tics, other movements, such as rocking, and many more behaviors. There are several reasons stimming can occur in children and adults with autism. Let's look at some of the main types of stimming and the possible triggers.

Hand flapping

Of all the stimming behaviors, hand flapping is perhaps one that is most noticeable in children with ASD. It is a type of repetitive behavior that can occur for short or long durations.

Hand flapping can present itself as a stimming behavior in many ways, including:

- Moving fingers vigorously
- Clicking fingers
- Moving arms

Most of the time, hand flapping is nothing to worry about and the behavior can be triggered by any of the following:

- Excitement
- Nervousness
- Fidgeting
- Decreased body movements

Hand flapping is only a cause for concern if it results in **self-harm** or gets in the way of the child's daily living, through limiting the use of his/her hands.

Verbal and auditory stimming

Auditory stimming is any repetitive behavior that has the potential to impact on a person's sense of hearing or effective communication. It may include:

- **Repetitive speech** (learned words such as song lyrics, movie lines, book passages)
- Covering or tapping of ears, snapping fingers, or tapping on objects repeatedly
- Humming, grunting, or high-pitched noises

Visual stimming

Visual stimming is a behavior that is connected to a person's sense of sight. It may include:

- Staring blankly at objects

- Hand flapping (as described above)
- Lining up objects such as toys
- Blinking repeatedly
- Turning lights on and off

Tactile stimming

Tactile stimming refers to repetitive behaviors connected to a person's sense of touch. Examples may include:

- Rubbing or scratching hands or objects
- Repetitive hand motions such as opening and closing fists.
- Tapping fingers repeatedly
- **Tactile defensiveness**
- **Holding hands and fingers at an angle**
- **Arching back while seated**

Vestibular stimming

A vestibular stim is a behavior linked to a person's sense of balance and movement. It may include:

- Rocking back and forth or side to side
- Twirling or spinning
- Jumping repeatedly
- Hanging upside down

Olfactory or taste stimming

Olfactory stimming centers around a person's sense of taste and smell. It includes repetitive behaviors such as: smelling, licking hand or tasting unusual objects.

Tantrums

A tantrum is an outburst that happens when kids are trying to get something they want or need. Temper tantrums are typical for toddlers and preschoolers. Once kids have more language to express themselves, tantrums tend to subside a little. But some kids are more prone to tantrums even after those early years. They continue to be impulsive and find keeping their emotions in check challenging. They may get angry or frustrated quickly.

Kids with these challenges might have a tantrum if they don't score in a game of kickball, for example. They may get upset when siblings get more attention than they do. Yelling, crying, and lashing out aren't appropriate ways to express feelings, but it's happening for a reason and kids ultimately have some control over that behavior.

Kids may even stop in the middle of a tantrum to make sure the parent or caregiver is looking at them and then pick up where they left off. The tantrum is likely to stop when kids get what they want—or when they realize they *won't* get what they want by acting out.

Meltdowns and Strategies

A meltdown is very different from a tantrum. It's a reaction to feeling overwhelmed. For some kids, it happens when they're getting too much sensory input— that's information coming in from their senses. Kids may become upset by certain sounds, sights, tastes, and textures. This is called **sensory overload**.

The commotion of an amusement park might set them off, for instance. For other kids, it can be a reaction to having too many things to think about. A back-to-school shopping trip could cause a tantrum that triggers a meltdown. A meltdown is a reaction to trying to process too much sensory input all at once. Too much sensory input can be overwhelming—not just for kids, but for adults, too. Here's one way to think about too much sensory input.

Imagine filling a small water pitcher. Most of the time, you can control the flow of water and fill the pitcher a little at a time. But sometimes the water flow is too strong and the pitcher overflows before you can turn the water off. That's how a meltdown based on sensory overload works.

The noise at the amusement park or the stack of clothes to try on in the dressing room at the mall is sensory input that floods the brain. Once that happens, some experts think the "fight-or-flight" response kicks in. That excess input overflows in the form of yelling, crying, lashing out, or running away—or even just shutting down completely.

The causes of tantrums and meltdowns are different, and there are strategies that can help stop each of them. A key difference to remember is that tantrums usually have a purpose. Kids are looking for a certain response. Meltdowns are a reaction to something. And even if they start out as tantrums, they're usually beyond a child's control.

Kids can often stop a tantrum once they get what they want, or when they're rewarded for using a more appropriate behavior. That's not the case with meltdowns. Meltdowns tend to end in one or two ways. One is fatigue, kids wear themselves out. The other is a change in the amount of sensory input. This can help kids feel less overwhelmed. For example, your child may start to feel calmer when you step outside the store and leave the mall. So how can you handle tantrums and meltdowns differently?

- **To tame tantrums, acknowledge what your child wants without giving in.** Make it clear that you understand what your child is after. "I see that you want my attention. When your sister is done talking, it'll be your turn." Then help your child see that there's a more appropriate behavior that will work. "When you're done yelling, tell me calmly that you're ready for my time."

- **To manage a meltdown, help your child find a safe, quiet place to de-escalate.** "Let's leave the mall and sit in the car for a few minutes." Then provide a calm, reassuring presence without talking too much to your child. The goal is to reduce how much information is coming in. Watching your child have a tantrum or a meltdown and worrying about other people's reactions can be stressful. It may help both you and your child to know that these behaviors are common, and they can improve.

Chapter 5

Indicators of Development

Understanding behavior can be very complicated for a parent of a special needs child. Sometimes there needs to be a guide to help a parent to know if there are behaviors that need to be paid close attention to. Below are a series of questions under different categories that parents can use to get an idea of a child's capacity to hear, understand and respond to different cues. After each series of questions, you will have an opportunity to take notes of what you observed, and you may want to share with a teacher, physician or caregiver.

Communication

1. When you ask your child to point to her nose, eyes, hair, feet, ears, and so forth, does she correctly point to at least seven body parts?

2. (She can point to parts of herself, you, or a doll. Mark "sometimes" if she correctly points to at least three different body parts.)

3. Does your child make sentences that are three or four words long:

4. Without giving your child help by pointing or using gestures, ask him to "put the book on the table" and "put the shoe under the chair." Does your child carry out both directions correctly?

5. When looking at a picture book, does your child tell you what is happening or what action is taking place in the picture (for example, "barking," "running," "eating," or "crying")? You may ask, "What is the dog (or boy) doing?"

6. Show your child how a zipper on a coat moves up and down, and say, "See, this goes up and down." Put the zipper in the middle and ask your child to move the zipper down. Return the zipper to the middle and ask your child to move the zipper up. Do this several times, placing the

zipper in the middle before asking your child to move it up or down. Does your child consistently move the zipper up when you say "up" and down when you say "down"?

7. When you ask, "What is your name?" does your child say both her first and last names?

Gross motor

1. Without holding onto anything for support, does your child kick a ball by swinging his leg forward?

2. Does your child jump with both feet leaving the floor at the same time?

3. Does your child walk upstairs, using only one foot on each stair? (The left foot is on one step, and the right foot is on the next.) She may hold onto the railing or wall. (You can look for this at a store, on a playground, or at home.)

4. Does your child stand on one foot for about 1 second without holding onto anything?

5. While standing, does your child throw a ball overhand by raising his arm to shoulder height and throwing the ball forward? (Dropping the ball or throwing the ball underhand should be scored as "not yet.")

6. Does your child jump forward at least 6 inches with both feet leaving the ground at the same time?

Fine motor

1. After your child watches you draw a line from the top of the paper to the bottom with a pencil, crayon, or pen, ask her to make a line like yours. Do not let your child trace your line. Does your child copy you by drawing a single line in a vertical direction?

2. Can your child string small items such as beads, macaroni, or pasta "wagon wheels" onto a string or shoelace?

3. After your child watches you draw a single circle, ask him to make a circle like yours. Do not let him trace your

circle. Does your child copy you by drawing a circle?

4. After your child watches you draw a line from one side of the paper to the other side, ask her to make a line like yours. Do not let your child trace your line. Does your child copy you by drawing a single line in a horizontal direction?

5. Does your child try to cut paper with child-safe scissors? He does not need to cut the paper but must get the scissors to open and close while holding the paper with the other hand. (You may show your child how to use scissors. Carefully watch your child's use of scissors for safety reasons.)

6. When drawing, does your child hold a pencil, crayon, or pen between her fingers and thumb like an adult does?

Problem solving

1. While your child watches, line up four objects like blocks or cars in a row. Does your child copy or imitate you and line up four objects in a row? (You can also use spools of thread, small boxes, or other toys.)

2. If your child wants something he cannot reach, does he find a chair or box to stand on to reach it (for example, to get a toy on a counter or to "help" you in the kitchen)

3. When you point to the figure and ask your child, "What is this?" does your child say a word that means a person or something similar?

4. When you say, "Say 'seven three,'" does your child repeat just the two numbers in the same order? Do not repeat the numbers. If necessary, try another pair of numbers and say, "Say, eight two.'" (Your child must repeat just one series of two numbers for you to answer "yes" to this question.)

5. Show your child how to make a bridge with blocks, boxes, or cans, like the example. Does your child copy you by making one like it?

6. When you say, "Say 'five eight three,'" does your child repeat just the three numbers in the same order? Do not repeat the numbers. If necessary, try another series of numbers and say, "Say 'six nine two.'" (Your child must repeat just one

series of three numbers for you to answer "yes" to this question.)

Personal-social

1. Does your child use a spoon to feed herself with little spilling?

2. Does your child push a little wagon, stroller, or toy on wheels, steering it around objects and backing out of corners if he cannot turn?

3. When your child is looking in a mirror and you ask, "Who is in the mirror?" does she say either "me" or her own name?

4. Does your child put on a coat, jacket, or shirt by himself?

5. Does your child take turns by waiting while another child or adult takes a turn?

6. Do you think your child hears well?

7. Do you think your child talks like other children her age?

8. Can you understand most of what your child says? If not, explain:

10. Can other people understand most of what your child says?

If not, explain:

11. Do you think your child walks, runs, and climbs like other children his age? If not, explain:

12. Does either parent have a family history of childhood deafness or hearing impairment?

13. Do you have any concerns about your child's vision? If yes, explain:

14. Has your child had any medical problems in the last several months? If yes, explain:

15. Do you have any concerns about your child's behavior? If yes, explain:

16. Does anything about your child worry you? If yes, explain:

Chapter 6

Classroom Stories

Matthew

Matthew was 19 years old and in a class that was preparing him to transition out of 12th grade. He was nonverbal except for the utterances he would speak when trying to talk. He only had two years left in public school and he would have to leave the school and remain home. When I first met him, I noticed he was such a handsome boy, with deep blue eyes that he seemed to look all the way through you when he looked at you. He had the most wonderful smile that would brighten up a room when he was happy. Matthew was known as someone who was highly volatile when he became agitated about something. When he became agitated, he was known to suddenly start making humming noises. He would get out of his seat and start walking back and forth, rubbing his hands. He had been known to strike other children and even push adults out the way who seemed to be in his space.

In fact, many adults were afraid of him. I noticed that just from the tasks that I would give him, he would quickly complete them and the more analytical they were (puzzles), the faster it was that he completed them. After he completed a task, he quickly looked for another one to do, so this was an indicator to me that he was very high functioning. I found out that Matthew loved Cheerios. And so, I would always keep a small zip lock bag full of them in my drawer just in case he needed something to help him calm down. When it seemed as if he was starting to get on edge, I would ask him if he wanted some Cheerios. He would stand up and come over to the desk and put his hand out with a big smile and I would hand it to him. It made sense.

We started to communicate. He would mimic with utterances what he wanted to say. in one-word responses. He was unable to completely say a complete sentence, give directions or express his needs. One day I gave him a 60-piece puzzle. Usually when you give a child a puzzle, they first look at the picture and then they put the pieces together. But Matthew was different, Matthew put the pieces together and then looked at the picture. Yes, he was analytical alright and this was great. Eventually, the puzzles became more advanced, and I noticed that he loved doing them.

One day I had the bright idea that if he could put puzzles together, then he could put small wooden kits together. I went out and purchased a model airplane kit that was made of thin wood. Of course, after he put it together, he would have to paint it, which he really liked, and he was able to do it so quickly. In fact, in one day it was done. Even though he was nonverbal, he understood, and he could do a skill that many of the other students could not do. He was never anxious or showed signs of nervousness.

Eventually I left school and the next year, I questioned what happened to Matthew. I was told that he no longer attended the school. He was being homeschooled because he had attacked one of the teachers. Of course that saddened me. I realized that students develop relationships with their caregivers, their teachers, their support systems, and once it is developed it becomes their security. They learn how to trust. even if it makes them uncomfortable, and in their own way they learn how to love. In my heart I believed that Matthew missed me, and I could still see those blue eyes looking at me.

Little John

Little John was a second grader who was very, very bright and was on the higher autism spectrum. He had excellent communication skills. He could talk to you about anything. He was very highly functioning. He came to my class to practice reading. The rest of the time he was in a regular classroom. He would come down to my class for one hour and then return to his classroom. His teacher began sending me emails saying that when he returned from my class, he would refuse to do any work in her class. In fact, he would say out loud that he had finished the work for the day.

Little John was very astute to what fairness was, and what was being done justly in the classroom among all children, especially among himself. He would oftentimes remind the teacher if she did something for one student and not for another. He especially would remind the teacher when she did not do it for him. Every Friday we had something called "treat day," and on that day, if the students had a point given to them each day for good behavior, then on Friday they got a treat. They were able to watch a movie and receive a bag of potato chips and juice. Little John loved treat day. He would often talk to himself out loud. He would rationalize every situation out loud so as not to lose a point towards treat day. He would tell himself out loud to sit up and listen. He would say," I can't lose a point today."

He had a difficult time being reprimanded by teachers. When corrected, he would begin saying aloud that he hated school, and he hated the classroom. He would say, "I am never coming back, today is my worst day.". He would go on repeating the same thing until he got a response. He would disrupt the entire classroom and soon would have to sit in a quiet area to calm down and he never did, not on that day!

He was such a wonderful character. I remember at a parent's meeting I told his mother that when he was absent from school it really made me sad because he was so delightful and always had a conversation to share. When Little John misbehaved in class and did not get his point for that day he would go to the calendar and count the days left before treat day. He knew that he only had four more days left. Before it was "treat day." He would quickly ask if he could do any extra work so that he could get his point back

At the end of the week, it was fascinating to see how a small bag of potato chips and a juice box could mean so much. I realized that it is just the little things you do that make a difference and make children know that you care. I miss my little John.

Andre

He was 18 years old and academically tested on a first-grade academic level. He was a tall boy around 5'10" tall and weighed at least 200 lbs. His mother always described him as her big baby. In fact, she would say, "That's my big baby." My job that year with Andre was to teach him a lesson with him staying on track for 5, 8, and eventually 10 minutes, without having a tantrum, throwing things or overturning a table. He was at home this year, learning virtually and so his mother was a part of our teaching-learning sessions. In the beginning, his mother would say he did not know how to write or perform academically, that he was too low.

Eventually she allowed me to teach him and we began see an improvement with his time on tasks. Andre could speak. And he could tell you if something was hurting him. He could tell you if he was happy. He could express all kinds of emotions, and he had lots of tantrums all the time because he was used to not working. So, when I began teaching Andre, I started teaching him in small increments and when he completed the task, we celebrated it.

He was still a bedwetter and it had become a major chore now for his mother to care for him because of his size. His tantrums became more alarming because of his strength. I spoke to his mother and asked her the question, 'Who will take care of Andre, if something happens to you." She immediately began to cry and said that she thought about that often because she had a lot of health issues.

I knew I had to get the best I could from Andre for that year that I was going to be with him. I knew that I needed to try and get him as independent as I could. Eventually it was recommended that she contact social services and let a caregiver come over and assist her three days a week with Andre. He did learn how to write his name. He learned how to count and how to put things in order. He learned categories, compare / contrast, alike and difference. This made me happy because I knew he had experienced success and liked the feeling. I hope he is well.

DR. TERITA F. GUSBY

Chapter 7

Engleman's Syndrome: A Mother's Story
by
Dr. Fidaa Yousef Ahmed Diab

My daughter Rawda was born on 12-19-2023. She is my third child. I noticed at birth that she was different from my other children in her physical shape, eye color, and hair. She was named after her grandfather's name. I realized that she had difficulty eating and so I had to feed her from the very beginning and continued to do so. I knew it was a common thing for babies to cry but Rawda cried a lot more than normal. She weighed 6 pounds by the time she was 4 months old which was the same weight at birth. This baffled me.

I did not understand why she was not growing. I did not understand the delay. When I went to the doctor and was not able to get a clear answer, I then visited the American Hospital in Dubai. The daughter asked me, "When did your daughter laugh?"

I was very surprised at the question and had not given it much thought before. I was then asked the question again while we were traveling abroad to do a genetic test that at the time surprised at the request from the doctor, that we have one done.

Ten days later after the testing I was asked to return to get the results along with her father. At the time my husband was traveling and so I returned to the doctor alone. My husband could not be there in person but was on the telephone while the doctor and I spoke. It was very shocking news. I was told that my daughter suffered from a pathological condition of a GI Promotor Gene. The doctor first listed several of the positive effects and then continued explaining the more difficult ones. As she explained the condition, I found myself in a state of complete shock. I asked myself, "Is my beautiful child sick? Will this condition affect her all her life?

The meeting with all the information left me in a daze. I left the office and went out to my car. The doctor walked behind me carrying my child in her arms. When I got home, I had finally calmed down but was still amazed. I did not know exactly what to do. I sat in the room with my other three children. I began talking to myself as I realized the new journey that was in front of me. I realized that my daughter needed me to be strong. I cried the first day which I needed to do and then the journey began. I did not read about the disease, but I wanted to improve my daughter's health, as she is of low weight.

I stayed home from work for two months while I was feeding my daughter to improve her weight. After two months, I found that my daughter had difficulty sitting independently so I went to visit an orthopedist to ask why she lacked the ability to sit alone. He told me that my daughter needed intensive physical therapy. I then went to one of the specialized centers for physical therapy. She participated in intensive physical therapy sessions daily for three years.

Every day for three years, I went to this center after dropping my other children off at school and sat for three hours with my daughter in physical therapy. It was my daily routine. In the afternoon, after picking my children up from school we would return home. When returning home we met with a speech therapist as well as an occupational therapist. We were getting into a routine. But something happened one day when my daughter was two and a half years old.

One day when coming home with her I entered the house and placed her on the floor to play. After placing her on the floor she passed out. She did not move. I suddenly became alarmed. I did not know what was happening. I grabbed her and took her to the emergency hospital as quickly as I could. I found out that this was another result of the disease. My daughter had an epileptic seizure. The doctor performed an electroencephalogram on her so that he could confirm the presence of an epileptic seizure. After it was confirmed, I was then given special medications to stop them. My daughter suffered with these seizures until she was ten years old.

. I started supporting mothers who had the same condition as my daughter and other cases. My motto has always been acceptance, learning, and education. I accept my daughter. I'm learning to understand her behavior. "Learn until you get better."

I suffered. One of my challenges was to understand my daughter's needs, as she is a child who does not speak, laugh, nor cry. Eventually I learned that with time and learning, I was able to understand my daughter, and she does now speak what she wants. She participates in occupational speech therapy as well as attending a swimming academy. She understands love and returns it to her family and others who have shown love to her. It was difficult to find out what she wanted. But in discovering her wants and needs, I realized that she understands 2 languages. Our home is bilingual. She has a great memory of people and places. I discovered that earlier in her growing up that she could recognize streets leading to our home and became anxious when approaching them.

She continues to have difficulties when sleeping. She is unaware of danger and dangerous situations. Several times, she has tried to run away from the house not knowing the danger outside. I have had to always provide close and continuous supervision of her.

A Letter to my daughter-

To my daughter Rawda-

I have learned a lot from you. I learned to accept, help, and teach you. I learned to be proud of you, my daughter, Rawda. You taught me patience, my daughter. You taught me a lot by being patient. Despite this disease and all its problems - when I look into your eyes, I feel happy. I love your kind heart.

-Your Mother

Chapter 8

Picky Eaters / Nutrition
by
Natalie Pelton

Hello most amazing families,

When Dr. T asked me to write this chapter in her book, I was very excited to share not just my academic knowledge to help your kids thrive within her learning program but also my personal experience so you would know that your child can have one of the brightest futures you imagined for them.

I thought I would start off by introducing myself to let you get to know about the quirky (and hilarious) person who's going to teach you a completely different approach to supporting your child's autism.

An upgraded treatment than anything offered in a therapy office, but one that will enhance their brain development for better memory, better self-regulation, and even help them (in many cases) acquire speech in nonverbal cases. My promise to you, if you put in place the simple teachings I provide, is that you will not only have a happier child but also a more academically brilliant child as well.

But first…

How did I come to want to be here in this moment, sharing these very words with you?

My life prior to having a child with autism was a life of parties, late nights, take out foods, no exercise (except CPR), and a career that was demanding both on my mind and body. I was a front-line healthcare worker trained in trauma, OR, and angiography. In a nutshell, I was trained to look good at keeping my cool, even when people were coming in with traumatic injuries. You can say that now that I've left healthcare, I get to reap the benefits of PTSD worthy of army men on the battlefield.

Why do I share this? Because it was around the time of my 8th year in healthcare that I got pregnant, something that I never thought I wanted or would happen. But there I was, madly in love and ready to start a family. I also am sharing this because a deregulated nervous system like mine was not the prime host for pregnancy. My dreams became like many of yours.

A life of watching my little ones take their first steps, say mama, and eat ice cream on hot days together while I put band-aids on the little scrapes they got from falling doing something mind-blowingly fun, except that's not what happened.

I had also just had an operation for a kidney stone removal at 8 months pregnant, on morphine and antibiotics for a week prior because, of course, no one wants to do surgery on a pregnant lady. I went back to work with a tube in my kidney and forced myself to work. A month later, when I was coughing profusely because of a cold (during the H1N1 scare no less), my water broke. My son was born perfect in every way after 28 terrible hours of labor. He did all the most amazing things. He hit milestone after milestone, until he didn't. He spoke a few words, and then they disappeared.

At 18 months old, we were at the family doctor for another antibiotic prescription for yet another chest infection for my son when she voiced her concerns on his speech. Roughly a month later, I sat in my new pediatrician's office expecting a speech therapy referral but was completely blindsided by what she told me. Her very words were, "Yup, I'm almost positive your son has autism." Cue in all my motherhood dreams ripped away from me. In my defense (for such a drastic reaction), is the fact that I had been in healthcare for 10 years, and my only experience with special needs children was that of severe kids that were suffering.

My lens of the world associated autism with suffering because that is all I saw and knew. I have learned over time that this is not necessarily the truth, but back then… my motherhood and my child's future were stripped away in one simple sentence. Plus, if I'm truly honest with you all, my journey with autism was that of suffering. It did not disappoint. From a broken elbow to constant infections. From nosebleeds to bumping into everything. To never knowing if my child would be able to communicate basic needs to others was the world, we lived in. Eloping was a thing for us, and once my child almost got hit in the parking lot when he ran away from me as a car backed up.

If you're reading this and you're new to your autism diagnosis, don't worry; it's not all doom and gloom that I'm going to share. I'm going to do the opposite. I'm going to tell you there's hope for a completely different outcome, even if you've been told otherwise.

- ✓ My son at 5 1/2 could not say words, let alone a sentence or even consider conversation.
- ✓ My son at 7 1/2 was released from all care and deemed no longer to need a diagnosis.

What happened within those two years is what you're going to find within these pages.

How is This Related to Food?

Picky and Sensory Eating………. the Dilemma

As an autism mom and nutritionist, I understand the challenges you face when trying to get your child to eat healthily. One day they may enjoy chicken nuggets, and the next day, they toss them on the floor for the dog. Trust me when I say, you are not alone. One of the most common issues I see in kids with ASD is picky eating and a strong addiction to sugar. Correcting this not only benefits their academic performance (yes, you can raise your child's IQ with food), but it also completely transforms the lives of families within the home.

In the following pages, I'll delve into lifestyle practices that support better focus, emotional regulation, and memory. But right now, you may find it hard to believe that your child could incorporate such foods into their diet. You might have given up on certain foods a long time ago or never even tried them because they're not part of your own diet. Fear not, as I'm about to share a 3-step process that I know works wonders in overcoming picky and sensory eating, along with a crucial strategy to keep in mind during implementation. No secrets here. Below is the 3-step process in order:

1. Overcoming the Resistor Stage: We focus on what's currently working and meet our kids where they are at, especially if they seem to refuse everything else and stick to a specific brand of food for all meals.

2. Helping Your Child Become an Adventurer in Their Nutrition Journey: Creating a safe environment during meals and fostering connections, relationships, and celebrations around food can make it not only seem safe but also exciting and pleasurable. The introduction of food chaining has also simplified this process.

3. Introducing More Bitter Foods: We'll explore the most researched and successful way to do this—using negotiation. Learn how to effectively negotiate using healthy favorites as an exchange for less loved but equally healthy foods.

You may have heard that it takes introducing a new food eight (8) times for a child to try it, but in my experience, some foods required way more than 20 introductions, in various forms and ways. Patience and perseverance are key, and you'll be amazed at the progress your child can make on their nutrition journey." You might feel like time is a luxury you don't have, just as I did initially. However, I soon discovered that appointments for ear infections, chest infections, speech-language pathology, assessments, doctors' visits, and hospital visits were the real time drains.

But when I invested my time in food introductions, I significantly reduced these visits. As a full-time shift worker with a side business, if I could do it, so can you.

Why do toxins matter?

Due to liability reasons, I can't delve too deep into toxins and detoxification because of client advice and everyone is unique, but I can educate. In our toxic world, over 80,000 chemicals created by humans make life easier, with few tested for safety, leaving us vulnerable.

Pesticides like Roundup frequently hit the headlines for liability losses and cancer-causing trials. Shockingly, the World Health Organization found over 200 chemicals, some causing developmental issues and deformities, in women's umbilical cords. Chemical toxicity might be linked to the severity of autism. That's why, in my Blue Life Autism Program, "Building Brilliant Brains for a Better Tomorrow," we guide kids through four detoxes: chemicals and liver support, heavy metals in our food, mycotoxins like mold, and gut health, which we know is interconnected with autism.

What are "crap" foods and why should they be absolutely avoided especially during school time?

    Carbonated drinks

    Refined sugars and flours

    Artificial colors, sweeteners and alcohol

    Processed anything.

As a mom and nutritionist, I want to talk about anti-nutrient foods, which are harmful to our children's bodies and deplete their nutrients while providing little to no nutritional value.

First, let's look at carbonated drinks, commonly known in

different parts of the country as "pop." This includes beverages like Root Beer, Sprite, Mountain Dew, Canada Dry, Pepsi, and Coke. Even non-sweetened carbonated drinks can be harmful due to the presence of chemicals that our children may struggle to process, leading to chronic illnesses and reduced life expectancy.

Next, we have refined foods, which are foods like white rice, white bread, and white sugar. Fruit juices often fall into this category too. Gluten and refined flour can act as opioid-like substances in your child's brain, impacting their focus, especially during school. Many foods that have been altered from their original whole food form are also considered refined, like peeled potatoes or bananas.

Artificial colors and flavors are common additives found in fruit juices, candies, fruit rollups, breakfast cereals, and other children's favorites. These additives are known as neurotoxins that can impede sensory processing and brain development. When combined, their toxic effects can increase significantly.

Processed foods are another concern. While eliminating them

may seem daunting, it's essential to find nourishing replacements for these items. Processed foods include potato chips, store-bought baked goods, packaged items with unknown ingredients or non-natural preservatives, frozen foods, and more. I understand it might feel overwhelming, but it's essential to implement changes gradually. Replace unhealthy options with nourishing alternatives.

Our children's brains may be conditioned to seek out salt, sugar, and fat, but with the right approach, we can help them develop healthier eating habits. Picky eaters, who often crave processed foods, can also overcome their habits through the process I teach. Stay tuned for the next part of this chapter, where I will delve into practical strategies to support your child's brain development and address sensory and picky eating habits. Remember, small steps can make a big difference in creating a healthier and happier future for our kids.

Unfortunately, some physicians claim that food doesn't impact autism, but I beg to differ. After all, autistic kids are still human kids, and nutrition affects all children. I work closely with physicians, including my business partner, an emergency physician certified in lifestyle medicine. The good news is that physicians are continually growing in their knowledge of autism, microbiome, nutritional deficiencies, and toxicity. I've witnessed this shift firsthand, with sought-out pediatricians in neurodevelopmental disorders eagerly seeking to learn about my approach to treating severe and high-functioning autism.

When I talk about lifestyle medicine and my methods, the first question I get from physicians, parents, therapists, and family members is, "How do you get them to eat the food?" To address picky eating, it's crucial to understand the science behind it.

Surprisingly, in the third trimester, babies can actually smell the perfume their mom is wearing or the garlic from the pizza she's eating, a phenomenon called olfactory labeling. Furthermore, flavors from the food a pregnant woman eats goes into the amniotic fluid, impacting the child's taste preferences. This process doesn't end in the womb.

Even a mother's breast milk changes in flavor based on her diet, giving the baby more exposure to different flavors and potentially making them less picky eaters. In a study, children exposed to varied diets during infancy had lower chances of developing food rigidity, rejection, and neophobia (fear of new foods). Although some picky eating tendencies may be genetic, children can be taste trained into enjoying nutritionally dense foods, even if they initially avoid slightly bitter vegetables.

Parental modeling plays a crucial role in children's food choices and eating behaviors. It's essential for us to lead by example and create a positive influence on our kids' diets. Marketing and cartoon influences on unhealthy foods are prevalent, but as parents and caregivers, we can make a difference in our children's nutritional habits.

What is Neophobia?

I have had the opportunity to work with many families facing the challenges of food neophobia in their autistic children. Food neophobia is not simply a case of picky eating; it goes far beyond that, representing a complete aversion to trying new foods. This can be an especially distressing situation for parents as they witness their child's limited diet and the potential impact on their health and well-being. Fortunately, I have witnessed firsthand that food neophobia can be overcome with the right strategies and patience.

As a nutritionist, my approach is rooted in the belief that food should be seen as an exploration and an adventure, rather than a source of stress or pressure. When approaching the world of nutrition with autistic children, keeping this framework in mind becomes the cornerstone of the journey toward improved eating habits. I want to delve deeper into the three stages that I've mentioned before: the resistor stage, the adventure stage, and the negotiator stage. Each of these stages plays a vital role in helping children gradually expand their food preferences and develop a healthier relationship with food.

The Resistor Stage:

During the resistor stage, children display extreme rigidity in their food choices. They might have a rotation of only 1 to 10 different foods, and these foods are often tied to specific brands, textures, or presentations. For example, a child might only eat chicken nuggets from a particular company or refuse to eat yogurt unless it is a specific brand.

This stage can be concerning for parents as the child's diet becomes severely restrictive, leading to potential health issues such as constipation or diarrhea. In extreme cases, children may even require feeding tubes as they refuse food, resulting in a decline in their overall health and an increased risk of developing chronic illnesses or mental health issues.

As a nutritional therapist, I believe that the best approach to start with is using what already works for the child and making it exciting and fun. Engaging and encouraging the use of the same foods that are accepted, but with minor changes, can be a great starting point. For example, introducing breakfast for dinner or cutting preferred foods into different shapes can add an element of novelty. Food fading is another technique that can be useful during the resistor stage. It involves incrementally changing the food by 10% or less to encourage acceptance. For instance, if a child prefers white rice, slowly adding 10% quinoa or cauliflower rice can be a gentle way to introduce variety.

The Adventurer Stage:

The adventurer stage is where real exploration begins. While this stage may take longer to show progress, it is essential for creating lasting success and forming new, healthy habits. During this stage, the focus shifts to the concept of food chaining.

Food chaining involves introducing foods that are similar to the child's preferred ones but have slight differences. For example, if a child enjoys chicken nuggets, you can gradually introduce baked or grilled chicken. This approach helps the child feel safe and curious about trying new foods, as they are still close to what they already enjoy.

10 Food Chaining Examples

1. If the picky eater likes chicken nuggets, gradually

introduce baked chicken tenders, then roasted chicken, and eventually grilled chicken.

2. For a child who enjoys cheese pizza, try adding a small number of vegetables like bell peppers, onions, or mushrooms as toppings and increase the veggies gradually.

3. If the picky eater likes pasta with butter, try mixing a little marinara sauce with the butter and slowly increase the amount of sauce.

4. For someone who enjoys plain yogurt, introduce a small amount of fresh fruit or a drizzle of honey, and then increase the amount over time.

5. If the picky eater enjoys French fries, introduce sweet potato fries and then baked sweet potato wedges.

6. For a child who likes peanut butter sandwiches, try using almond or cashew butter, and later introduce different types of nut or seed spreads.

7. If the picky eater enjoys apple slices, try offering other

fruits with a similar texture, such as pear slices, and gradually introduce different fruits.

8. For someone who likes grilled cheese sandwiches, try adding a small amount of spinach or other leafy greens between the cheese slices and gradually increase the greens.

9 If the picky eater enjoys plain rice, try adding a small number of mixed vegetables and gradually increase the vegetable content.

10. For a child who likes plain oatmeal, try adding a few berries or diced fruit and slowly increase the variety and number of fruits.

I understand that it can be tempting to insist on the child trying new foods repeatedly, as we often hear that a child needs to try food up to eight (8) times before accepting it. However, for a child with autism, this number can be much higher, sometimes upwards of 20 times. Additionally, communication challenges and sensory issues can make the process more complex.

Therefore, patience and a non-judgmental approach are crucial during the adventure stage. It's essential to celebrate every step of progress during this stage, from just looking at a new food to actually taking a bite and swallowing it. **<u>Creating a positive and joyful mealtime environment is key to encouraging acceptance of new foods.</u>** Celebrate even the slightest engagement with the new food, such as touching, smelling, or licking it, as these are all steps towards progress.

<u>The Negotiator Stage</u>:

The negotiator stage should only be introduced once the child is comfortable with the adventure stage. In this stage, a "bite for bite" system is utilized. The child is offered a bite of the preferred food followed by a bite of a new food. Gradually, the ratio of new food to preferred food is increased until the child is comfortable eating the new food on its own. The negotiator stage empowers children to taste-train themselves with familiar flavors but at a more conscious level than the resistor stage. It is essential to use negotiation tactics carefully to avoid creating unhealthy food habits. Starting this stage prematurely or overusing it may lead the child to expect only preferred foods, making it challenging to introduce new foods later.

Throughout the entire process, a multi-system approach is crucial. Continue with the strategies mentioned in the previous stages, ensuring that each step is demonstrated or described above is maintained. Remember that every child is unique, and progress may vary. Each small achievement should be celebrated, and mealtimes should be made enjoyable rather than stressful.

I have found that incorporating juicing and popsicles can be an effective way to introduce new flavors while still appealing to the child's preferences. Juices made from fresh fruits and vegetables can be frozen into popsicles, offering both a sweet treat and essential nutrients. At the Blue Life Autism program, we provide multiple smoothie and juicing recipes to assist families in moving in the right direction. The program offers support through weekly calls and tailored approaches to fit each family's lifestyle and needs.

Overcoming food neophobia in autistic children requires dedication, patience, and a positive mindset. By embracing food as an exploration and adventure, we can gradually expand children's food preferences and create healthier eating habits. Celebrating every step of progress and maintaining a safe and familiar environment are essential elements in this journey.

Remember, the goal is not just to get the child to eat new foods but to develop a positive and joyful relationship with food that nourishes both the body and mind.

Building the Brilliant Brain and raising your child IQ

If you have a picky eater, you have the opportunity to introduce foods that can support their developing brain, giving you an advantage over most parents, even those with neurotypical children. As their brains and neuroreceptors develop at a younger age, our children have different nutritional needs than we do.

You may be surprised to learn that nutrition can have a significant impact on the brain. After food is absorbed, it affects brain functioning through four main classes of functioning compounds:

- ✓ Energy for the brain, also known as glucose.
- ✓ Building blocks such as lipids, fatty acids, and amino acids.
- ✓ Bioactive molecules with multiple brain actions, including epigenetic regulation.
- ✓ Micronutrients for enzymatic and hormonal processes.

There are powerful nutrients and minerals that can help our children raise their IQ and academic performance, building brilliant brains. Essential vitamins like vitamin C, found in citrus fruits and Kiwis, and vitamin B, present in green vegetables, animal foods, and eggs, play a crucial role in brain development. Essential minerals like zinc found in beans can also support brain function.

Neurotransmission speed, referring to a child's capacity to receive and make sense of information, can be improved through nutrition. Many children with autism suffer from processing disorders, and nutrition can positively impact their brains.

Zinc is an essential mineral that can aid neurons in forming neural synapses, resulting in better connections and pathways. Conversely, deficiency can interfere with neural pathway formation and neurotransmission, leading to attention deficits, reduced brain activity, and decreased fine and gross motor skills.

Autistic children often test lower than neurotypical children in these areas. To improve child brain development, prioritize foods high in recommended nutrients:

Zinc-rich foods: sesame seeds, buckwheat pasta (boiled), lentils (boiled), eggs (boiled), green peas (cooked), turnip greens (cooked), avocados (raw), and kale.

- Vitamin C-rich foods: currants, raw kale, raw Kiwi fruit, raw cauliflower, raw Brussels sprouts, raw chestnuts, boiled broccoli, raw green peas, and raw kidney beans (or in flour form).
- B vitamins are also crucial for brain health, and here are five of the most common deficiencies found in autistic children:

- B12-rich foods: Salmon, lamb (cooked), eggs, turkey, chicken, and trout. Plant-based or vegetarian children may need B12 supplementation, as it's often derived from animal sources.

- Folate-rich foods: sunflower seeds, raw spinach, boiled asparagus, raw beets, raw arugula, broccoli, mixed nuts, raw kale, raw Brussels sprouts, and raw cauliflower.

- B3 (Niacin)-rich foods: tuna fish, dry-roasted non-GMO and organic peanuts, chicken breast, salmon, Portobello mushrooms, almond butter, sprouted peas, baked potatoes (with skin), raw green peas, and raw black beans.

- B1-rich foods: non-GMO corn flour, raw black beans, all nuts, raw soybeans (non-GMO), raw green peas, raw garlic, boiled asparagus, broccoli, and dried currants.

- B6-rich foods: raw garlic, boneless beef, sunflower seeds, baked potatoes, hazelnuts, salmon, raw black beans, raw cauliflower, raw Brussels sprouts, and raw spinach.

Many of these foods contain multiple B vitamins, making it

easier to prioritize and provide a variety of nutrients for your child. Remember, introducing these foods should be done gradually, following the picky eating strategies mentioned earlier. Removing harmful foods should also be a priority. Excessive consumption of added sugar, trans fats, and artificial colorings has been shown to have harmful effects on both learning and behavior.

Therefore, it's essential to focus on a balanced and healthy diet. One powerhouse nutrient for cognitive development that can significantly impact all areas of improvement is omega-3 fatty acids. By incorporating these nutritional strategies into your child's gluten and dairy-free diet, you can support their brain development and help them thrive in various aspects of their lives.

Nutrition practices for attention and concentration

As a mom who is also a nutritionist, I can't stress enough the importance of a well-thought-out nutrition plan when it comes to enhancing attention and concentration in children. One of the primary factors to consider is the impact of blood sugar spikes and dehydration on a child's ability to focus and learn effectively. It's quite surprising how much of an impact sugary drinks and snacks can have on a child's attention span. No matter how nutritious the meals may be, if your child is still consuming juices and sugary treats throughout the day, it can lead to fluctuations in blood sugar levels, resulting in attention loss or difficulty focusing on school.

Equally significant is the role of hydration in cognitive function. The brain is comprised of roughly 73% water, making proper hydration essential for optimal brain activity. Factors such as body weight, activity level, and climate influence a child's daily water needs, which increase as they grow older, ranging from approximately 1.1 to 2 liters a day.

Here are the rough estimates of children's water intake by age.

- ✓ A child that is one to two years old should be drinking 1.11 liters to 1.33 liters daily
- ✓ A child that is 2 to three years old should be drinking 1.33 liters to 1.38 liters daily
- ✓ A child that is 326 years old should be drinking 1.38 liters daily to 1.5 liters daily

- ✓ A child that is 6 to 11 years old should be drinking 1.5 to 1.7 liters daily
- ✓ A child that is over 12 years old should be drinking 1.7 to 2 liters daily.

To ensure your child is getting enough water, involve them in choosing a water jug they love that contains the required daily amount and is easily accessible. Gradually increasing water intake, whether it's by a few hundred milliliters each day or every other day, can ease the transition to proper hydration. Incorporating low glycemic foods into your child's diet can also have a positive impact on their focus and concentration.

Low glycemic foods, which release sugar more slowly into the bloodstream, help maintain stable blood sugar levels throughout the day, leading to better sustained attention. You can find the glycemic index online, and by focusing on consistent low glycemic choices, you can contribute to improved sleep quality and concentration during school hours.

High glycemic index foods, on the other hand, have been

shown to negatively affect attention. Cereals, pop tarts, and sugary pancakes or waffles are common examples of high glycemic foods to avoid. Instead, consider options like steel-cut oatmeal or poached eggs served with low glycemic veggies and no starch.

Dear Amazing Parents,

Congratulations on taking the first step to support your children's brain development and sensory challenges! This enhanced grocery list is designed to provide essential nutrients that contribute to healthy brain function and neurotransmission. By incorporating these foods into your children's diet, you can help them reach their full potential, improve memory, focus, and overall brain health:

Fresh fruits like apples, pears, and berries are also excellent low GI choices due to their fiber content, which slows down sugar absorption. For healthy and low glycemic snacks, you can offer your child fresh fruits paired with unsweetened yogurt or introduce them to pumpkin seeds, sunflower seeds, hemp hearts, or almonds, which not only provide essential nutrients but also boost focus with their omega-3 content.

It's crucial to be mindful of hidden sources of added sugars as well. Often, sugars are present in unexpected places like ham, salami, seasoned peanuts, certain bread types, flavored water, vitamin water, energy bars, and even some salad dressings.

Being aware of these sources and avoiding them whenever possible will contribute to your child's overall health and concentration. As you embark on reducing your child's sugar intake, it's essential to understand that they may experience withdrawal symptoms. While there's no one-size-fits-all solution, gradually removing sugary foods and drinks from your home can help them adjust better. Within a couple of weeks, you will likely notice positive changes in your child's behavior and focus as their body adapts to a healthier diet.

Lastly, it's important to recognize that the nutrients essential for brain development are equally crucial for memory and learning. By providing a balanced diet rich in essential nutrients, including omega-3 fatty acids, vitamins, and minerals, you will support your child's overall cognitive function and academic performance, leading to a more focused and successful learning experience. My goal is to help you lay the foundation for your child's health and well-being, ensuring they thrive both academically and in all aspects of life.

Below is a list of some of the best brain nutrient foods

Enhanced Grocery List for Brain Development and Sensory Support:

- egg yolks, soybeans, mustard, sunflower seeds, fatty fish (e.g., salmon, anchovies, sardines)
- PS: fish (fatty fishlike salmon), beans, most meats, egg yolks

- DMAE: salmon, anchovies, sardines
- PCA: unprocessed foods (fruits, vegetables, meats, chicken, fish)
- Vitamin B5: mushrooms, eggs, avocados, peas, lentils, tomatoes, cabbage, celery, alfalfa sprouts
- Vitamin B1: beans, peas, lamb, asparagus, watercress, mushrooms, cauliflower, Brussels sprouts, lettuce, peppers, cabbage
- Vitamin B12: tuna, turkey, chicken, egg yolks, shrimp, lamb
- Vitamin C: broccoli, peppers, watercress, cabbage, cauliflower, strawberries, tomatoes, kiwi, citrus fruits, peas, melons

I understand that the journey of supporting children with sensory processing disorder and autism can be challenging, and I am here to offer my support and expertise. Over the years, I have dedicated my life's work to helping autistic children thrive, find joy, and embrace their unique gifts. If you would like further assistance or wish to work with me, please visit my website at *www.blueliferx.com*.

Better yet, I encourage you to watch my informative webinar and join my program *at www.blueliferx.com/autismwebinar*. I am passionate about getting to know each one of you and your children personally and guiding you towards a healthier, happier, and more vibrant life. Wishing you an exciting journey of learning and growth with Dr. T and her wonderful academic learning program.

Together, we believe that every child has the potential to thrive, grow, and make a positive impact on the world.

With warm regards,

Natalie

DR. TERITA F. GUSBY

Chapter 9

Housing and Special Needs / Under the Foundation
by
Danielle Terrell

The structure of this chapter includes the following information:

- History: U.S history of residential programming
- Trends and Issues in Housing
    - Wait lists for long-term services.
    - Waitlist for support services.
    - Funding and Costs of Living
    - Access to services
- Types of Residential Programs
- Environment
- Caretakers
- The Foundation: Action Steps for Planning

- On the other side of the fence: summary of residential program models in other countries

Every person comes from a different home. Every home is built from a foundation. Under the foundation lies a story, for some the story is solidified through generations. When you open a door to a home, you may find many things just as unique as the people living inside them. For a child with autism, like any other child, their home may change as they grow. The dynamics, the walls, the photos on the mantle, the people in and out of the home. As the child grows up depending on their needs their childhood home may become a residential school (depending on their needs).

A home may become an apartment, an assisted living facility or group home. There are many types of homes and many possibilities for autistic children, and it is never too early to start searching for housing options. Even if you never imagine your child living outside of the "family home" consider the following. After all, you don't know what you don't know. There are many things to consider when defining independence for your loved one and thinking about future planning.

No matter what stage of planning you may be in, always keep paper and electronic files of your child's official diagnosis. These documents will be important throughout your child's life and may be a requirement for provider agencies to offer residential opportunities.

Autistic individuals should be able to choose where they live and, in an environment, where they can thrive. Depending on their level of independence throughout life, they may need continuous support from their family to find an affordable house that can best support their wants and needs. People with disabilities have the same basic rights as other members of their community and have the right to participate in choices and decisions that affect their lives, such as choosing housing.

History: U.S History of Residential Programming

Caretaker *nouns* "one that gives physical or emotional care and support." Caretaker *noun* "one that takes care of the house or land of an owner who may be absent." Caretaker *noun* "one temporarily fulfilling the function of office. According to the dictionary, Merriam-Webster, the word caretaker, was first used in 1801.

The 1800's reveals much about American history and the lives of people with disabilities. At this time, the towns in colonial America were responsible for the care of individuals with disabilities. When overcrowding and unregulated conditions became too much the state government took responsibility. Facilities became homes for individuals with disabilities, known as asylums and state hospitals. Treatment facilities in America sometimes used European hospital adaptations to support individuals. From the 1960s to 1990s, many American hospitals and psychiatric institutions closed and changes in treatment of individuals with disabilities shifted (Meldon, 2017). From 1977-1998 the number of state operated institutions declined and over 100,000 residents moved to community based residential settings.

Residents went from overcrowded living arrangements to living in settings ranging from 15 or fewer residents (Kim et al., 2001).

Due to higher rates of health complications, research shows that autistic individuals may be at risk of early mortality (Smith DaWalt, et. al., 2019). While it is known that often individuals with autism spectrum disorder have comorbid diagnoses, the healthcare field is advancing, and predictors of mortality have changed over the years. This leaves families with different questions, "Will I outlive my child?" "Who will take care of my child when I am gone?" "Will their siblings become their caretaker?" These are discussions that should be had with your family members and your community. In addition to advanced research and medical care, community-based care has also improved the quality of life and trends of longer life expectancies for adults with disabilities have been seen in the U.S.

According to an article published in 2018, 71% of individuals with intellectual and/or developmental disabilities (IDD) in the U.S. need a family caregiver. The role of family caregivers includes, but is not limited to, daily care needs, activities of daily living and service and care coordination. Across the United States, there are waitlists for alternative housing, and gaps in residential services thus the high rates of family support will continue to play a critical role for adults with IDD. The data from this article revealed that out of the adults with IDD receiving care from family caregivers, 27.27% are individuals diagnosed with Autism (Williamson, et., al. 2018).

The promotion of independence and community inclusion has helped foster different avenues of future planning for autistic individuals. Lack of alternative housing options forces the role of family caregivers to be critical throughout their lifespan. Reports have found that 54% of family caregivers have not developed plans including residential, costs, and special need trusts (Lee et al., 2020).

Caretakers

The sibling carer: in many families, the role of the primary carer transitions from parent to sibling. A 2014 study collected data from semi-structured interviews with adult siblings over age 40, 13% of the participants had an autistic sibling, while the others were siblings being cared for with other developmental and intellectual disabilities. The purpose of this study was to explore the transition of care, investigating circumstances, and experiences to understand the realities faced by sibling caregivers. Results from this study had three major findings with key themes supported by over 50% of the siblings in the sample. First was that families experienced ongoing modifications to their roles as caregivers as their siblings with a disability aged. Planning steps are vital to making needed adjustments in their lives as they transition to care for their siblings. Third is that the support systems around siblings contributed to the success of transition of care (Coyle, et al., 2014).

Caretakers can change throughout your child's life. Some families may experience home services inside their family home. Various therapists, tutors, and caretakers in and out of the house before and after school. Some children benefit from home schooling and have professionals in and out of family homes throughout the day. Knowing your child's support system and needs can help your child grow inside your home and in their community. As important it is to have unique, and qualified caretakers, the physical environment is also important to a child's success.

Environment

Sometimes autistic children and adults may experience a sensory overload. For some this can result in meltdowns, aggression, migraines, and even depression. Some home modifications can be simple while others may require additional funding and resources. Families can work with someone from their child's therapeutic team, like an Occupational Therapist to design sensory friendly, safe, and comfortable environments. Adjustments can be made throughout the lifespan depending on your loved one's needs. Creating a sensory-friendly home can help avoid sensory overload, significantly affect behavior, reduce irritability, stress and anxiety. Knowing your child's preferences and sensory experiences can help reduce sensory overload.

Some ways to stary modifying your home is to change the lighting. Some autistic people have difficulty processing visual input. It is best to allow natural light into the home while avoiding fluorescent lights. Window tinting and anti-glare coatings on windows may help as well.

Investing in sound-absorbing insulation may also be needed. Purchasing high-quality rugs can help minimize footsteps if your child benefits from pacing and you live in an apartment complex. Alterations to windows can help minimize external sounds. Loud noises can be upsetting to anyone, a white noise machine, or noise-cancelling headphones can also help.

Smart devices that can help with temperature regulation can provide several benefits to your child's health, behavioral and emotional status. Children and adults can also benefit from a sensory room. Some families may choose to do this with a basement, garage, or extra bedroom. A tactile-friendly environment can help stimulate your child's needs. Adding swings, water tables, ball pants, bean bags, lights and sound machines can help an individual throughout their day or be a safe space for meltdowns. .Limiting fragrances throughout a home can also benefit autistic people. Avoid harsh cleaning products, candles, and room fragrance sprays. However, you create this space, ensure it is inviting, and comfortable, and can start with once space. Small spaces can also promote your child their own personal space or adults with their own private space to indulge in sensory-seeking behaviors. Sometimes this sensory area can even be outside. Don't forget about ensuring safety measures are also implemented inside and outside the home.

Laws, Regulations, Federal Programs, and Human Rights

Fair housing laws create integrated, community-based housing options for people with disabilities, non-discrimination laws, and housing protections across living environments. Housing choice impacts individuals' access to job opportunities, community resources, healthcare, and education, and it affects overall physical and mental well-being.

Professionals such as, but not limited to, teachers, direct support professionals, case managers, and physicians are trained mandated reporters. This is a legal obligation that if any mandated reporter suspects abuse, they are required to report it to the appropriate state agency.

Americans with Disabilities Act (ADA) "Title II of the ADA covers housing provided or made available by public entities (state and local governments and special purposes districts). Title III of the ADA prohibits private entities that own, lease, and operate places of public accommodation from discriminating based on disability and requires places of public accommodation and commercial facilities to be designed, constructed, and altered in compliance with established accessibility standards. Public accommodations at housing developments include any public areas that are open to the general public, such as a rental office. Public accommodations would also include, for example, shelters and social service establishments" (HUD 2023).

The Fair Housing Act of 1968 makes it illegal for housing providers to refuse to provide reasonable accommodation for individuals with disabilities. Social Security Act of 1935 established benefits for persons with disabilities passed by President Franklin D. Roosevelt. In 983, Congress added section 1915(c) to the Social Security Act, giving states the option to receive a waiver of Medicaid rules governing institutional care. This is when Home and Community Based Services (HCBS) first became available. In 2009, nearly one million individuals were receiving services under HCBS waivers. Within federal guidelines, states can develop these waivers to meet the needs of people who prefer to get long-term care services and support in their home or community (Medicaid.gov).

The Rehabilitation Act of 1973 prohibits discrimination based on disability in programs conducted by federal agencies. Section 504 of the Rehabilitation Act and Americans with Disabilities Act – Section 504 requires that recipients of federal financial assistance ensure that their programs and activities are readily accessible and available by individuals with disabilities. Title VIII created the

Independent Living Services and Centers for Independent Living programs (ACL, 2020). "Title VII, chapter 1 of the Act states the current purpose of the program is to "promote a philosophy of independent living including a philosophy of consumer control, peer support, self-help, self-determination, equal access, and individual and system advocacy, in order to maximize the leadership, empowerment, independence, and productivity of individuals with disabilities, and the integration and full inclusion of individuals with disabilities into the mainstream of American society.""" (ACL, 2023).

Olmstead v. L.C. (1999) allows people with disabilities to live in the least restrictive settings possible that meet their needs and preferences. The Section 811 Supportive Housing Program for Persons with Disabilities program is a federal program that provides funding to developers of housing for disabled, low-income households. Frank Melville Supportive Housing Investment Act of 2010 is a federal program established to reform and revitalize the U.S Department of Housing and Urban

Development section 811 Supportive Housing for Persons with Disabilities Program.

Despite federal laws and regulations studies have shown that people with disabilities, compared to other protected classes, are more likely to experience discrimination when seeking housing. Continued advocacy to state representatives to expand its resources and access to high-quality, affordable homes is needed.

Trends and Issues in Housing

Significant trends in housing issues have included: decreasing large institutions and facilitating residential settings through community integration, decreasing out-of-home placement of children and youth, and increasing independence through self-owned or rented homes (Lakin et al., 2007). Having adequate funding and access to affordable housing is a continued trend seen throughout the U.S for decades. The cost for families supporting a child with autism per year, is averaged at $60,000 (Breslow, 2019).

Funding and Costs of Living

In 2013, the state of Florida estimated a total of $4.02 billion was spent on long term care (Braddock, 2015). In 2013, the United States spent $157.4 billion in long term care from federal disability funding through home and community-based services waivers.

A 2019 article in Autism Spectrum News reported that over the next decade the Center for Disease Control and Prevention estimates that 500,000 teenagers with autism will age out of their school-based services. In the absence of adequate government support, private sectors throughout the country are developing. Findings related to the average costs to place and care for someone in a group home is approximately $90,000 to $140,000 per year (Breslow, 2019).

Types of Residential Programs

"Under Section 504 of the Rehabilitation Act and the Americans with Disabilities Act, recipients of HUD financial assistance, state and local governments, health care facilities, group homes, assisted living facilities, colleges and universities, and housing rental and sales offices, among others, have the legal obligation to take appropriate steps to ensure effective communications with individuals with disabilities" (HUD, 2023).

It is important to note that living environments and residential programs vary from state to state. This includes definitions of different supported and independent living environments, licensures, cost, availability, and services. Determining a good fit for a home also varies from individual to individual. It is essential to visit, tour, and research housing options. It is also essential to connect with local parent resources and information centers. Compliance and implementation of policies may also vary from state to state and may depend on federal requirements.

Parents and caregivers should research how their state defines group living, what certifications exist, zoning laws, and which state agencies license homes and facilities. For example, the State of Massachusetts (MA) does not allow "congregate housing" and certifications for group living arrangements are verified by 8 different state agencies in MA. The Executive Office of Health and

Human Services supports individuals with disabilities through various departments and services.

However, when the Autism Omnibus Bill was introduced and passed the state omitted supporting housing options for people diagnosed with autism. Therefor in some states, an extra step by caretakers to find alternative housing options. In the state of New York, the Office for People with Developmental Disabilities addresses housing-related programs. The California Department of Housing and Community Development

Key words for your housing search

Group homes assisted living facilities, skilled nursing facilities, independent housing programs, community habitation, family care, paid neighbor, supportive housing programs, in-home services, centers for independent living.

Centers for Independent Living (CIL) are designed and operated by individuals with disabilities, found across the United States. To receive funding, states must submit a State Plan for

Independent Living (SPIL). This plan is then monitored by a Designated State Entity to ensure each independent entity monitors, revies and evaluates the implementation of the SPIL. A list for centers for Independent Living by state can be found in an A-W directory by visiting the Administration for Community Living's website. Each program allows people with disabilities to live with dignity, make their own choices, have access to tools, resources, support in their community, make their own choices, and promote self-determination, and equal opportunities (ACL, 2023).

Financial Resources

Affordable housing projects and campaigns allow for the preservation and development of affordable living options. Family, advocates, and other caretakers can support autistic individuals by applying for affordable housing. Assistance can also be provided by seeking rental assistance programs, independent living skill programs, seeking housing with environmental modifications, access to community resources, utility assistance programs, assistive technology and more.

Subsidized housing is a government rental assistance program that provides people with low incomes to find affordable rent-based housing. Reduced rents can be found online through participating housing communities. Each property will have its own system for accepting applications and may have waitlists.

Housing choice vouchers, or Section 8, is a national voucher, that can pay for all or part of rent. Eligibility is based on annual gross income, and family size and are limited to U.S citizens and non-citizens who have eligible immigration status. Your local housing agency can also support individuals with how to apply and check the status of an application. Once a child turns 18, it is recommended that they apply for a Section 8 housing voucher and/or local housing voucher program. Due to the shortage in resources the waitlist for the programs can range from two to ten years.

Public housing is designed for people with low incomes, and individuals with disabilities. These homes range from single-family houses to high-rise apartments. Public housing differs from state to state. Contact your location Public Housing Agency to learn what documents you need to apply and other requirements for eligibility.

Preservation of Affordable Housing (POAH) is a national non-profit organization that serves communities by providing rehabilitation, preservation, and rental assistance services. The Consortium for Citizens with Disabilities (CCD) is the largest coalition of national organizations working together to advocate for children and adults with disabilities. The CCD has a housing task force that focuses on protecting the rights of people with disabilities.

Additional National Housing Resources

Department of Housing and Urban Development (HUD) provides state and local governments funding for fair housing. Going online to resources.hud.gov you can find various resources, including finding a HUD office near you, affordable housing opportunities, local public housing, homelessness resources, affordable elderly, and special needs housing and more.

U.S. Department of Health and Human Services: Housing resources

Government

- Administration for Community Living
- Benefits.gov
    - Medicaid.gov
    - Home & Community Based Services
- USA.gov

Private and Non-Profit

- The Arc
- Autism Housing Network (AHN)
- Autism Society
- Autism Speaks

- Coalition for Community Choice (CCC)
- Global Leadership Institute
- The Kelsey
- Madison House Autism Foundation (MHAF)
- Technical Assistance Collaborative (TAC)
- Easter seals

The Foundation: Action Steps for Planning

The foundation starts with you! Act now, start planning, and remember you are not in this alone, have conversations with family members, your community, and other stakeholders. The continued collaboration of local, state, and national organizations are needed to lead efforts in advocacy and policy reform to social problems. Historically family members have been the catalyst to radical changes in policy and service delivery.

Throughout your child's life it will be important to foster independence and help them develop daily living skills. Independent living skills are a variety of skills such as problem-solving, personal care, communication, decision making, financial literacy, budgeting, self-care, and hygiene that should be learned to help a child or adult with autism live more independently. Continue to develop these skills throughout your child's life.

Prepare for transitions early, service network changes drastically during transitions especially after a child graduated from high school or their services through the Department of Education end.

Five important steps to consider for planning and assessing your child's skills. Look to your medical professionals, network of therapeutic supports and department of special education. After assessing skills, identify different levels of needed support. Next, start applying and get on waitlists. Third, apply for benefits, these are typically accessed around age 18-22. Research what is covered in your state's HCBS Waiver program. Invest time in person-centered planning. Future planning may also involve implementing legal formalities such as writing a will. Increasing knowledge about care providing programs and residential services has a positive impact for families and aging autistic people.

Chapter 10

Traveling with Autism

Travel presents a multitude of barriers connected to an individual's own profile – not everyone's needs are the same. All human beings are unique, after all. <u>Accessibility</u> – meaning an environment that is designed to be used by people with disabilities – also means different things to different travelers. Accessibility means having information clearly communicated and broken up into smaller pieces, rather than bunched together. It can mean providing quiet rooms to allow escape from noisy environments. It can also mean that airport, railway, or hotel staff are trained in ways to assist autistic people and avoid triggers, such as forcing eye contact. Accessibility has only recently begun to improve for autistic travelers and still has a long way to go.

Because so many people with autism experience hypersensitivity to noise, busy environments are a challenge, such as a shop where there are a lot of people, loud music, announcements, and so on. Going through security is not fun – especially when the social expectations are not clearly spelled out. TSA agents tend to be loud and forceful because of the numbers of passengers they must safely get checked in through security. This can be daunting to a person with autism who has a problem with crowds as well as the busyness associated with security check points. It is an alarming experience for people without autism.

Here's how to help an autistic person you're traveling with. If the child becomes fidgety and overwhelmed do not shout or tell him to calm down. It can be frustrating to be told that. Autism does not come with an "off" switch! If we can't speak coherently (or at all), still listen – even if we are in the throes of a meltdown, or we don't seem to be acting normally. We can't always tell you what the problem is, which is why avoiding potential triggers always helps. Don't force eye contact, which can be very uncomfortable for us. Helping us manage through confusing environments can go a long way, as well as ensuring our sensory needs – i.e., not too much noise – are being met. You can do that by learning the layout of airport or train terminals or finding out about what accessibility adjustments the venues offer. If you need to change a plan, be clear and upfront about it.

- Travel with a sensory kit. Think ear plugs, fidget toys etc. Fidget toys such as tangles can provide extra emotional regulation in an overwhelming environment; they allow the child to cope more easily for just that little bit longer. Keep sensory aids handy in your handbag or attached to a lanyard.

- Use a timetable as a form of itinerary. It's helpful to see the transition between tasks or activities – making sure you have enough time to get somewhere, change train platforms, and so forth – and tick everything off. This helps reduce stress if the planned routine suddenly changes.

- Never be without your mobile phone. If you need help, you can call one of the people you know and interact with most.

- Preparation and careful planning are crucial for ensuring a successful family vacation, regardless of the season when including an autistic or special needs family member. Without proper preparation, even to the smallest of details, the stress levels for parents- particularly with autistic children can be significantly heightened. To facilitate a smoother travel experience for families with autistic members, here are some helpful tips:

- <u>Accessibility</u> – meaning an environment that is designed to be used by people with disabilities – also means different things to different travelers. Accessibility means having information clearly communicated and broken up into smaller pieces, rather than bunched together. It can mean providing quiet rooms to allow escape from noisy environments. It can also mean that airport, railway, or hotel staff are trained in ways to assist autistic people and avoid triggers, such as forcing eye contact. Accessibility has only recently begun to improve for autistic travelers and still has a long way to go.

Because many autistic individuals have hypersensitivity to noise, busy environments are a challenge, such as a shop where there are a lot of people, loud music, announcements, and so on. Going through security is not fun – especially when the social expectations are not clearly spelled out. **Wearing a lanyard** enables airport personnel to recognize that you have a hidden disability without you needing to declare it. This allows you to travel independently through the airport whilst knowing that if you need any additional support during your journey, any personnel will be able to support you.

Before the flight

Create a social story.

In the weeks leading up to your trip, create a picture and/or word social story with your child that overviews the air-travel process. Include pictures and/or descriptions of security, the terminal, the airplane, the baggage claim, and so on. Include sensory experiences the child might encounter such as "ear-popping" at take-off and landing. Review this "travel book" as often as possible prior to **departure. This will help to increase predictability for your child in an otherwise unfamiliar process.**

Mark it on a calendar.

A few weeks prior to travel, hang a calendar with the departure date clearly marked and have your child check off each day until departure. Utilizing a calendar presents the concept of time in a concrete and visual way and may help your child to prepare for when a change in their routine will occur**.**

*If possible, do not wash any comfort items before travel. Traveling on an airplane can be overwhelming to the senses to any traveler, let alone to a child with ASD. Having a favorite item that smells like home, such as a blanket or a plush toy, can be soothing in such an environment.

Pre-pack meals and snacks.

There may be a limited assortment of foods offered in the terminal or on the airplane. This can prove troublesome if your child has any dietary restrictions or if your child is a picky eater. In light of this, it may be helpful to pack a variety of snacks and mini meals for your child. Also, remember to pack chewy foods, like fruit gummies or a bagel, for a child who seeks sensory stimulation orally.

Exercise prior to departure.

Traveling on an airplane involves long periods of being quiet and sitting still. Encouraging high motor activity prior to leaving for the airport will help your child to relieve any bottled-up energy before getting to the airport. High gross-motor activities, like running or jumping on a trampoline, for approximately 20 minutes are examples of ideal activities.

Have your child explain the process to you.

Once you have taken the time to prepare your child for travel, encourage him or her to explain the process to you, or to his or her toys. This technique can demonstrate how much of the traveling process the child has grasped and will expose areas where the child is not secure or still has questions. This approach should be tailored to meet your child's developmental level. For example, for a child with strong verbal skills, ask the child to explain verbally or through drawings what the travel day will look like. For a child who uses a "speaker box," program the device to have pictures of the different steps of the day (e.g., getting in the taxi, checking in at the front desk). It may be helpful to prompt your child if they forget to cover a topic (e.g., "Tell me about boarding the plane").

Airport security

Accommodation

To accommodate persons with disabilities, the Transportation Security Administration (TSA) has **established a protocol that allows for special accommodations.**

Do a practice run.

Contact your local airport to see if TSA will allow you and your child to do a practice walk-through of airport security. This may help the child become familiar with the airport security process prior to the day of travel.

Twice a year, American Airlines partners with Clearbrook, an organization that serves more than 8,000 people with disabilities, to host their Airport Experience and Mock Flight, a popular volunteer-led, semi-annual event at O'Hare International Airport that provides a full airport experience to children with autism and their family.

Role-playing alternative to a practice run.

If your airport does not allow for an actual practice run in the facility, or for you to take photographs or videos, role-playing at home is an adequate alternative. At home, you can take turns pretending that you or your child is the TSA officer, and the other is the person walking through security. It will be most beneficial to your child if you are as detailed as possible (e.g., ask your child to take his or her shoes off when appropriate).

On the airplane

Boarding.

Notify the gate attendant that you are traveling with a child with an ASD, and you will be allowed to board early or board last depending on your preference. Advantages of boarding early include not needing to wait in line at the gate or on the airplane while other passengers take their seats. Advantages of being the last to board include not needing to wait in line at the gate, not needing to wait in your seat while other passengers aboard the plane and being on the airplane for a shorter period.

Ear-popping

To prevent discomfort in the ears during take-off and landing, pre-emptively encourage your child to suck on a piece of candy or chew a piece of gum. If your child is unable to safely suck on candy or chew gum, a chewing toy can also be effective towards reducing ear-popping.

Watching the time

Placing a digital clock or a count-down timer in front of your child may help your child to know how much longer he or she can expect to be in-flight for.

In-flight entertainment

Allow your child access to items in their travel bag. Allow your child to have access to movies, iPods, books, coloring books, toys, etc. If your child enjoys tactile stimulation, they may benefit from playing with play dough or putty while on the airplane.

Check out these tips from our Integrated Pediatric Therapies therapists for ways to make the trip easier and fun for the entire family!

- Pick out 10 words about the trip (nouns, verbs, and descriptors - they should describe the sensory experience). Depending on your child's level of understanding, the words may be all nouns or a combination.
- Create a bin that can be explored before the trip. Kids will have familiar activities to play with in the car or on the plane.
- Bring along a comfortable toy, blanket, or stuffed animal. The trip may be a new experience, and having something that is familiar can be comforting.
- Look through pictures of previous trips and remind your child about the people he will meet, places the activities he may be doing while there. For example, pictures of an

airplane, car, hotel, cabin, beach, park, or museum. Each picture can also be paired with a simple label.

- Before your vacation, take a few day trips to places such as a zoo, museum or beach. You will learn which strategies worked well for your child. It will help you be more prepared for what you may need on a long trip.
- Don't forget to pack several preferred snacks to enjoy while in the car or on a plane. Lollipops and chewy candies can help during takeoff and land when traveling on a plane.
- Airline flights can be disruptive and challenging for children with autism.
- These tips can help you prepare and make your family flight go smoothly.

Air travel can be difficult for seasoned adult travelers and even more taxing for children. For kids with **autism spectrum disorder (ASD)**, who bring their own unique sensitivities to airports and flying, the experience can be even more difficult.

At Marcus Autism Center, in Atlanta Georgia, they understand the special needs of children with autism and have made available these tips to help your family plan for a successful air travel experience.

Pack

Packing the right items to support your child's needs can make a world of difference when traveling.

- Don't forget to pack necessary coping or treatment items in your carry-on bag, like a change of clothes and medicines.
- Bring items to keep your child entertained. Be sure to pack your child's favorite toys, books, snacks, headphones, and plane-safe electronics. Keep in mind that there will be times when electronics may not be used on the plane.
- Have contingency plans for possible flight delays.

Ask for help!

Many airports and airlines have supportive resources and staff. Don't hesitate to ask for the help you need.

- Learn where you can find resources at the airport, such as customer assistance desks, quiet rooms, family-friendly bathrooms and sensory-friendly rooms.
- There are many support staff within the airport to assist your family. Ask for support or accommodation when you need it.

Whether your family travels by plane or **by car,** preparation and communication are key.

Chapter 11

Age transitions

Many adolescents with ASD have complex educational and health needs and will likely benefit from transition to adulthood planning and access to services and supports for people with ASD across their lifespans. Ensuring equitable access to services and support for all people with ASD during adolescence and transition to adulthood would help to promote overall health and quality of life for people with ASD across their lifespans.

A greater number of children identified with ASD has led to a growing interest in the transition to adolescence and adulthood. For most young people, including those with ASD, adolescence and young adulthood are filled with new challenges, responsibilities, and opportunities. However, research suggests fewer young people with ASD have the same opportunities as their peers without ASD.

- High rates of unemployment or under-employment
- Low participation in education beyond high school
- The majority continue to live with family members or relatives
- Limited opportunity for community or social activities—nearly 40% spend little time with peers

In addition, individuals with ASD may experience changes in their ASD symptoms, behaviors, and co-occurring health conditions during adolescence and young adulthood. These changes can affect their ability to function and participate in the community.

Activity Transition Strategies

Children with autism have the tendency to become fully engaged in an activity they like and are likely to become negatively triggered by transition (changing to a different activity). It's always good to plan, to be prepared and consistent. **Transitions are when children move from doing one activity to another.** If an activity is highly charged and the child is totally engaged; it is difficult to stop the activity immediately and switch to another. There are cures that can be implemented that can make change smoother. Home transitions can include waking up in the morning, getting groomed and dressed for school.

Fostering a smoother transition requires some special techniques, patience, and consistency. Children with autism tend to become fully engaged and more likely to be negatively triggered by a transition. It is always good to plan, to be prepared and consistent. The following strategies can aid in helping children to make smoother transitions without reverting to outbursts, tantrums, or noncompliance. These children typically are visual learners so the transition must be one that is visible to them.

A *poster board* helps the child to see the activities in order and teach the movement of activities in the order you want performed. It can have pictures representing the activities you want to perform. If the child has a difficult time in the morning routines, there can be pictures showing what he is doing. A picture of a bed, toothbrush, soap, washcloth, etc. For example:

DR. TERITA F. GUSBY

Morning Board Example

1.

2.

3.

4.

5.

1. Choose a transition object to be carried by your child when it is time to move to the next activity. The object can be a small ball, toy, book, crayon, etc. When moving from one activity to another the child picks up the object and takes it to the next activity. Placing the object in the child's hand signals that a new

activity is about to begin, and it reduces anxiety of stopping one activity abruptly and beginning a new one.

2. Hold up a colored sheet of paper (red) when it is time to stop an activity. When a new activity begins, hold up a green sheet of paper to begin the new activity.

3. Use a telephone alarm or egg timer to signal when an activity has ended. The alarm can be soft music playing or a ring tone sounding. The alarm must stay consistent. When the child hears the alarm, the adult tells them it is time to stop the activity. Eventually the child will stop the activity without the adult assisting.

4. If a child is working on an activity (coloring a sheet, putting puzzles together, etc.) there should be a container available that when done the object can be placed in the container to signal activity is complete to begin a new one. The container can rest in a specific area in the room or be passed to the student to place completed work or objects in. This can indicate the ending of one activity and the beginning of another.

5. Utilize the lights in a room. The adult turns the light off and then on again to signal the stopping of an event or that it's time to physically move from one room or activity.

Transitioning between activities or locations can be different for children with autism spectrum disorder. Anticipating some of the challenges and preparing ahead of time can help reduce friction. Families with multiple children often need to attend a school or sports activity and have the autistic child accompany them. To help the child transition to an activity that may be unsettling or not enjoyable, package a bag of preferrable items that are familiar (such as toys, snacks, etc.) to make them feel more comfortable at the event.

It is always a good idea to prepare ahead of time to help reduce the number of demands on the child during a transition. Having the child's clothes and food ready the night before can make a world of difference. Try to anticipate what may happen during an unexpected transition and plan accordingly. For example, if it is difficult for a child to leave school after watching television, then you may not have to allow them to watch television during the morning school preparation routine. You may want to save it for an after-school activity instead.

Chapter 12

Virtual Learning Help

Education Prescriptions is a virtual learning program for students to use in a home environment with a support lead person. The Education Prescriptions Learning System is composed of 3 kits representing abilities on different spectrums. Each kit is packed with 30 or more manipulatives that represent skills in writing, math, reading, and language arts.

Each lesson can be used for students who are at the lower end of the spectrum of achievement as well as children on the higher end. The lessons are created for student success and confidence achievement.

For more kit information contact:

https://educationprescriptions.org

DR. TERITA F. GUSBY

Kit 1 / Level 1

(Kit 1 / Level 1 -cont'd)

Skills Included:

- ➢ Matching
- ➢ Sorting Numbers / Objects/ Letters/
- ➢ Writing using hand muscles for control
- ➢ Counting Numbers / Objects
- ➢ Recognition of Letters / Sounds
- ➢ Eye – Hand Coordination Exercises
- ➢ Color Recognition
- ➢ Letter Recognition
- ➢ Learning Shapes / Sizes
- ➢ Writing / Identification of Name

DR. TERITA F. GUSBY

Kit 2 / Level 2

Children with Autism Learn Logic Reasoning, Skill Development and Self-Confidence.

Counting / Number Association Cutting / Coloring /

Pasting / Compare and Contrast / Matching

Addition / Subtraction /Writing Letters / Word Usage / Beginning Reading

DR. TERITA F. GUSBY

Kit 3 / Level 3

High School and Young Adults with Autism Transition to Preemployment and Post Secondary Training / Survival Signs/ Social Acceptance / Post High School Lessons /Money

For Teachers

Parents are your best source of information on the child's behavioral issues and the strategies they utilize at home that are effective. Like any student you teach, the child with autism will benefit most when the teacher and parent are on the same page and effort in the home and at school become mutually supporting.

Many children with special needs are no longer being taught in traditional classrooms around the country. After the Covid pandemic, many parents decided to keep their special needs children at home and homeschool them or allow them to receive virtual services though their school programs. Parents are their children's first teachers but specialized teaching for special needs students requires different methods and proven techniques to be able to see growth and development happening.

The Academic Learning System was developed during Covid specifically for special needs autistic children who needed hands on manipulatives to assist them in learning concepts and techniques in reading, math, and language arts and transitions at home as well as in a virtual setting. Included in this chapter you will find lesson examples that will allow a student to learn and achieve skills needed for lifelong learning.

Each exercise requires one-on-one adult supervision. The rule of thumb is very simple: "When a child has mastered a skill….move on, and when not mastered… teach again." Depending on the child, lessons should not last any more than 30 minutes. Some lessons will take fewer than that depending on the child's ability. Parent involvement is vital but remember that you must allow your child to independently learn a skill. Sometimes it is difficult to see a child do an activity wrong repeatedly but at a certain point, they will learn the correct way to solve the problem presented to them. Be patient. You will notice 2 different lessons in several exercises.

Consistency is vital in student learning outcomes. Repetition serves as a head coach. We want you to use these lessons for teaching and exploration enjoyment. Each skill your student successfully completes will enhance self-confidence and self-esteem. Teach repeatedly…it counts! Each lesson is presented within a 10–30-minute time frame. Do not over-teach. Move on to the next lesson if you find yourself losing your child's attention. Even though it is good to complete a task, you may find some days to be more challenging than others. Your student may want to perform a task several times, but it is okay.

These lessons are full of fun, mixed with mastery and meaningful instruction. Let's make this a great adventure in learning. The lessons following are ones on level 1. There is not a specific age for the lessons because child development happens to children at different intervals of development. There may be a lesson that a 7- year-old is practicing while at the same time a 11 year may be working on it as well. Lessons plans in schools are age and grade grouped.

DR. TERITA F. GUSBY

LESSON 1

EGGS UP / Math

Materials needed

1 empty egg carton

12 white ping pong balls

Instructions

Set the egg carton on the table in front of the student. (Model the activity first that you want performed.) The adult will place 1 ball at a time in each section of the carton. Start placement from left to right. Count aloud as you place a ball in each section. If verbal, allow the student to repeat counting. When you have placed all 12 balls in the carton, take them all out and say, "Now it's your turn."

Activity 1

1: Place your hand over the hand of the student assisting in picking up a ball and helping to place each ball in each section. Count each ball aloud as it is placed in each section. Continue until all 12 balls have been placed in the carton. Say "Good Job" and repeat the activity.

Activity 2

Allow the student to place each ball in the carton independently, starting from left to right. Assist the student in counting each ball as it is placed in the section. Now count and place balls in descending order beginning with 10, 9, ,8, 7, 6 etc. Say, "Good Job" and repeat activity.

DR. TERITA F. GUSBY

LESSON 2

COLOR MATCHING STICKS / Math

Materials needed

Pack of Mixed Colored Sticks

Instructions:

Place the colored sticks in a bag mixed altogether.

Activity 1

Adult places one stick of each color on the table one at a time. Say the name of the color aloud to the student, if verbal the student will repeat the name of the color. Adult reaches inside of the bag and places another sticks next to it of the same color. Adults help students find the same color stick to place on the table. Keep placing sticks until there are no more of that color left. The adult reaches into the bag to bring out a different color stick. Say the color aloud and if verbal, the student will repeat the color. Assist the student to find the same color that has been placed on the table. Continue until the sticks of that color are done. Continue activity with allowing students to reach in the bag and match the color laid on the table. When all sticks have been matched, say, "Good Job" and repeat activity.

Activity 2 Matching Sticks

Begin with reaching into the bag bringing out 4 different colored sticks. The adult will say the color name for each stick, if verbal the student will repeat. Have them spaced out on the table. Starting with the first color, have the student reach in the bag and pull out the corresponding color. Go on to the second colored stick and have a child match it with the others. Continue until all sticks are on the table and match up correctly. Say "Good Job" and repeat activity.

DR. TERITA F. GUSBY

LESSON 3

LETTER WRITING / Language Arts (Eye-Hand Coordination)

Materials needed:

Dry Erase Board / Marker

Instructions

Activity 1

Adult will take the marker and draw a straight line from left to right at the end of the board. The adults will place their hand over the student's hand and help the student trace over the line drawn. The adult will assist the student to make a second line under the top line in the same horizontal motion from left to right. Continue this process until five (5) lines have been drawn from left to right across (horizontally) the board. Erase the board and begin again using the hand over hand technique to help child trace a vertical line from top to bottom of the board. If necessary, assist the student in drawing five (5) more vertical lines on the board. This same technique can be extended to drawing circles, squares, and rectangles.

Activity2 / Letter Writing

The adult prints the student's name on the dry eraser board. The student traces and then independently writes the letter. The student writes his name 3 times on the board correctly. The student says each letter of his name as it is written. If nonverbal, the adult says the letter aloud as students write it. This activity can be extended for writing numbers, alphabets, simple words, color names, names of fruit, and shapes.

DR. TERITA F. GUSBY

LESSON 4

COLORED BALL LACING / PATTERNS / COLOR MATCHING

Eye Hand Coordination

Materials needed

2 Lacing Strings

Wooden Colored Balls

Instructions

Activity 1

An adult will introduce the student to one color ball at a time to be placed on the string. The adult will place a colored ball on the string. Adults will say the color name of the ball. The adult will say," find another _____ ball. All balls are to be placed inside of a plastic bag or container. With string in her hand, the student will reach into the bag or container and pull out the same color ball to place on the lacing string. This is repeated with the student until all the same color balls have been strung on the string. Adults choose different color balls and places on string. Student finds the new colored ball to place on string and laces all the new colored balls on the string. This is repeated until all balls have been strung on the string. Say "Good Job" and repeat the activity.

<u>Activity 2 / Colored Ball Lacing</u>

Adult will begin a two-color pattern with student (ex. Red, Yellow, Red, Yellow). The student will follow the 2-color pattern. When finished, the adult will choose another two colors to place on string. This activity can be progressed by setting up a pattern with 3 colors and then 4. If verbal, the student will repeat colors as she places them on the string according to the color pattern set up. The adults will instruct students to place each color on the string to form patterns.

LESSON 5

COLORING / Language Arts

Materials needed

Coloring Book

Crayons

Instructions

Activity 1

Students love coloring. This is an opportunity for your student to explore using eye-coordination to color a picture. The emphasis is not that he stays within the lines. The experience is using color to spread on a paper medium. You may want to have the student start with one color and then add another before the entire paper is covered. Adult will say "Good job" when student completes activity and display where student can see it.

Activity 2

If a student is familiar with different colors and has moderate eye-hand coordination, discuss colors and how they are represented on different objects. (For example: trees are green, bananas are yellow, etc.)

DR. TERITA F. GUSBY

LESSON 6

SORTING TIME / Language Arts

Materials needed

Plastic Cups /Colored Wooden Sticks

10 Colored Balls

10 Plastic Spoons

Instructions

Activity 1

This is a sorting lesson. Place 10 cups on a table or desk.

- From left to right, students will place 1 wooden stick in each cup.

- From left to right students will place 1 wooden ball in each cup.

- From left to right students will place 1 plastic spoon in each cup. Continue until each cup has 1 spoon in it.

Now in reverse order:

- The student will take a plastic spoon out of each cup.

- The student will take a wooden ball out of each cup. The student will take a colored wooden stick out of each cup. When cups are empty, the student stack each cup inside one another. Exercise is complete. Say to student, "Good Job" and repeat activity.

LESSON 7

ABC FLASH CARDS / Language Arts

Materials neeeded

ABC Flash Cards

Instructions

Treasure Hunt

Activity 1

Pull letters A B C D E F G out of the deck. Turn all the cards down on the table. Slowly lift the card up and tell what letter you see. (Say, "This is A" place it up on table.) Go to the next letter naming the letter until you have said each letter up to G and placed them face up on the table. Ask the student to pick up letter A. If he picks it up say, "Good Job" if he does not show you the letter "A" pick the letter "A" up and keep it in your hand. Ask the student to show you the letter "B" and so on until each letter is from the table and in your hand. Lay the letters out again and begin the lesson again.

Say the letter aloud. If a student is verbal, she should repeat the letter.

Activity 2 (Treasure Hunt)

Place all cards in a deck after mixing them up. Select a card, Turn it over. Look for something in the house that begins with the letter sound. Find it and bring it to the teaching area.

Activity 3

Place each letter face down and have students pick each one up and say the name of the alphabet. If she says the correct name, say "Good job." If she does not, continue to the next letter picking up letters and placing them in your hand until finished.

LESSON 8

MAKE IT COUNT / MATH

Materials needed:

Ping Pong Balls

Egg Carton

Instructions

Activity 1

The adult will shuffle the number cards. (1-5) Lay each card face down so as not to see the number on it. Turn a card over and say aloud the number on the backside of the card. Open the egg carton and count aloud the number of balls that are on the card. Place each ball (left-right) in each section. Clear the balls out of the carton and select another number card on table and repeat after you have turned over the second number card. Continue until all 5 cards have been turned over and balls placed in carton for each one. Tell the student "Good Job" repeat activity.

Activity 2

Continue this action using numbers (6-10) to fill up balls in the egg carton.

Activity 3

Combine 2 numbers together and add them. Place the balls in the carton to represent the numbers.

DR. TERITA F. GUSBY

LESSON 9

WOODEN SHAPES / Language Arts

Materials needed:

Wooden Shapes Puzzle

Instructions

Activity 1

The adult will place the wooden puzzle on the desk or table. The adult will name each shape along with the color (ex: yellow square). The adult will take each shape out of its holding area and set each one on the side of the board. The student will place each shape back into its cutout area. If the student needs assistance, please use the hand over hand method to assist student with pieces. SAY "Good Job" and repeat the activity.

Activity 2

The adult will place the puzzle in front of the student. The student will take each piece of the puzzle out from the board. The adult will call out the name of the puzzle (Say: Find the square) When asked the student will set each piece back into its correct space back in the puzzle. Say "Good Job" repeat activity.

LESSON 10

CAN YOU COUNT? / Math

Materials needed

Colored Wooden Sticks

Number Flash Cards

Instructions

Activity 1

Adult will place a number card face up showing the number on a table or desk surface. Assist the student to place one stick on the number 1. Take the card away. Place the card with the number 2 face up. Assist students to place 2 sticks on the card. Take the card away. Continue with the activity until you have used cards 1-5. Say "Good job" repeat the activity.

Activity 2:

Adult will repeat the same activity as above but will continue from 1-10.

Activity 3

Student will perform the activity again but go in descending order (10, 9, 8, 7 etc.)

LESSON 11

MAGNETIC LETTERS / Language Arts

Materials needed

Magnetic Letters Dry Erase Board or Refrigerator

Instructions

Activity 1

Introduction of alphabet. Adults will place each letter of the alphabet on desired surface and say each letter. If the student is verbal, they will repeat the letter. If nonverbal proceed with naming each letter.

Activity 2

Name Spelling. Spell out the name of the student on the surface. Naming each letter. Scramble the letters up and call each letter out and see if student can pick the correct named letter to spell his name. If done on the refrigerator it can remain visible.

LESSON 12

TWO AT A TIME / Math

Materials needed

Plastic Cups

10 Ping Pong Balls

10 Wooden Colored Balls

Instructions

Activity 1

Place 5 cups on a table or desk surface. Adults will model placing 2 ping pong balls in a cup. Students will place 2 ping pong balls in each cup. The student will then place 2 wooden colored balls in each cup. Students will remove 4 balls out of each cup one at a time until all the cups are empty.

DR. TERITA F. GUSBY

LESSON 13

MATCHING LETTERS AND CARDS / Language Arts

Materials needed:

ABC Flash Cards

ABC Magnetic Letters

Instructions

Activity 1

(Level 2 Activity) Adult will lay out each alphabet card on a table from A-Z with alphabet showing. Place the magnetic letters in a bag or container. Adults pick up a letter out of the bag and match it with the ABC flash card. Place the letter on top of the card to match it. Now it is the student's turn to select a letter out of the bag. The adult can assist in helping to match the magnetic letter to the flash card if student cannot do it independently. Continue until every letter has been matched.

LESSON 14

SORTING BALLS WITH EGGS / Language Arts

Materials needed:

Wooden Colored Balls

Egg Carton

Instructions

Activity 1

Take the egg carton and place it on the table. Place the wooden balls in a bag or container. Adults will select one color of the wooden balls to place in the first slot of the egg carton. Students will be guided to begin selecting balls of the same color to place in each section from left to right. After all the balls of one color have been placed in each slot of the carton, remove them and place them back into the container or bag. Adults will place a different color ball in the egg carton slot to begin the sorting activity again. The student will begin the activity by selecting the new ball color until all the balls of that color have been used. Continue activity again with a different color ball until every color has been sorted. Say "Good Job," and begin activity again.

DR. TERITA F. GUSBY

LESSON 15

CIRCLE SQUARES AND LINES / Language Arts

Materials needed

Dry Erase Board / Marker

Instructions

Activity 1

Using the dry eraser board, the adult will draw a picture of a circle. An adult will place her hand over the student's hand and direct him to trace the circle. The students and adult together, using this technique, will together practice drawing 5 circles. Erase board. Hand over hand, the adult will guide student in drawing a square. Together the student and teacher will practice tracking and draw 5 more squares. Continue this exercise with other shapes (lines, triangle, zigzag lines etc.).

Early Childhood Skills

Children at a very young age are familiar with learning the alphabet song or parents teaching numbers 1-10 by rote (saying them repeatedly). These are basic skills that young children entering school tend to be familiar with. When you have a child with a special need, it is not always the case that the child will enter school knowing some early childhood skills. Parents may encounter having a child who is nonverbal. How do you teach hm the alphabet, counting or the basic colors of crayons? You may have a child who lacks social skills and has difficulty being still in each space. When the child enters a classroom and is told where to sit in a particular seat, this may present a challenge because he may have freedom of movement at home, which is totally different at school.

Kindergarten readiness includes motor skills like holding a pencil and using scissors. Self-care, like getting dressed and not needing help in the bathroom, are important basic skills. So, let's start with the basics. The difference with special needs children is that you may find yourself teaching an early learning skill to a 13-year-old who before was not developmentally ready to learn it. The skill may be as simple as holding a pencil correctly with a tight enough grip to form letters.

Transition Writing Skills

Here are some basic transitional skills that are essential for students to grasp as early as possible towards independence:

Recognizing letters to write names.

Parents can use plastic alphabet refrigerator magnets to learn the letters of the alphabet. The next step is for the child to be able to recognize the letters that spell out his name.

Forming letters to write names (first and last).

It is easier to introduce writing starting with capital letters in the beginning and, if possible, introduce lower case letters after mastery of capital ones. For some students they will only be able to write their names in capital letters, which is okay. This process can be lengthy so the caregiver needs to be patient and understand that depending on the child it can happen within a short period of time or for months. Why is this skill important? Depending on the given situation, where a child may have to identify herself, writing down her name can be the difference between locating a parent or remaining lost. If you have a nonverbal child but she recognizes the question, "What is your name?" This will give her an advantage to maybe be joined with a parent. For those students who are developmentally able to correctly form letters, there should be a gradual emphasis placed on the following writing skills:

- First and Last Name
- Address
- Telephone Number
- Birthdate

In each scenario where a child may get lost and wander off from a parent or caregiver, you want that when found that he can give enough information to be returned to safety. Even though parents may not be able to foresee ever getting separated from their child, it is better to have a plan in place just in case it happens. Some parents have lanyards placed around a child's neck with an identification card with information on it if the child is nonverbal or lacks social skills.

In Conclusion

No one person or family should attempt to make difficult situations alone. The necessity of working with a team of people from the standpoint of both practicality and your own mental health is important. The problems we face, as caregivers, parents and as a society, dictate that we learn and produce better working together. What a blessing it is to use one another's expertise, to trust and depend upon one another and to form the mindset of support along the way. There is no way that we're going to be successful in our attempts to help children if energies, talents and information are not pooled together. Success in major prevention and growth efforts will never come about until the entire community becomes a part of the journey.

There are invaluable lessons in being a team. As we come together and exchange ideas, there is a sort of magic that takes over and spontaneous solutions begin to become planted and grow. Caregiving has its moments of becoming distressing sometimes, but the outlook looks brighter when we learn about the many others who have found solutions to get through and thrive. There exists an abundance of ways to provide services to children in need. We must also provide services for parents and caregivers too. These are healthy self-help models that do require commitment, leadership, flexibility, creativity and common sense.

The message of this book represents the commitment to provide some tools to begin the journey. We must ask ourselves, where are we now and where can we possibly go from here? With autism, the mentality of working as a village is one that is healthy and productive. As human beings, we must rely on one another to make it through this world. We were not all born the same way, we don't all function the same way, but if we are willing, we can live amongst one another peacefully and comfortably. We find out that sometimes things that are very different, when looked deep enough, have more similarities than we imagined.

Directory of Agencies And Organizations

DR. TERITA F. GUSBY

Autism Research Institute (ARI)

4182 Adams Avenue

San Diego

CA 92116

Autism Research Institute (ARI) is a nonprofit organization founded in 1967 by psychologist and **father of modern autism research**, Dr. Bernard Rimland. ARI provides both support networks and further research for both children and adults with autism spectrum disorders. Dr. Rimland and the Autism Research Institute have always believed that Autism is treatable. ARI's goal is to develop a known standard of care for everyone with autism spectrum disorders and the availability of resources for all families. "Research that makes a difference".

Web: http://www.autism.com

Email: cme@autism.com

Phone: 866-366-3361

Autism Science Foundation (ASF)

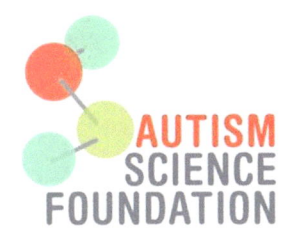

Suite #502,

28 West 39th Street

New York

NY 10018

The Autism Science Foundation is an Autism nonprofit organization founded by scientists and parents working together. The Autism Science Foundation provides funding to scientists conducting and disseminating autism research. They also provide information about autism to the general public to increase awareness of autism. Along with funding research, publishing their findings, sponsoring meetings and scientific workshops they provide <u>referrals</u> to support groups.

Web: http://www.autismsciencefoundation.org

Email: contactus@autismsciencefoundation.org

Phone: 212 391 3913

Autism Society of America (ASA)

4340 East-West Highway

Suite 350

Bethesda, MD 20814

The Autism Society of America is headquartered in Bethesda, Maryland. It is host to the most comprehensive national conferences regarding autism. The Autism Society of America is the nation's leading autism organization, which was founded in 1965 by Dr. Bernard Rimland and Dr. Ruth Sullivan who both have children with autism.

The Autism Society has a large network of affiliates allowing it to lead the way in state and local legislation regarding autism in the United States. In 1988 the Autism Society was the first organization to vote a member elected person with autism to their Board of Directors.

Web: http://www.autism-society.org

Email: info@autism-society.org

Phone: 1.800.328.8476

Autism Speaks, Inc.

1 East 33rd Street

4th Floor

New York

NY 10016

This is one of the top Autism organizations in the United States. Founded in 2005 by grandparents of an autistic child, Autism Speaks has become the world's largest, leading advocacy organization for autism. Founders Bob and Suzanne Wright along with a friend, Bernie Marcus, donated $25 million dollars dedicating this organization to fund research into causes treatment, prevention, and a cure for autism. Autism Speaks leads the way in 25 states to ensure that insurance carriers provide coverage for the necessary diagnosis, treatment, and therapies of those with autism.

Web: http://www.autismspeaks.org

Email: familyservices@autismspeaks.org

Phone: (888) 288-4762

DR. TERITA F. GUSBY

Birth Defect Research for Children, Inc.

976 Lake Baldwin Lane

Suite 104

Orlando, FL 32814

Birth Defect Research for Children, Inc was founded in 1982 and is a nonprofit organization dedicated to linking birth defects with their causes. Birth Defect Research for Children, Inc keeps a national registry and is available daily to provide support and contact between families with similar birth defects. This immediate and one on one referral system helps provide reassurance for many families dealing with disabilities. Studies are being conducted with regard to how our environment and the pollutants in our environment are linked to birth defects.

Web: http://birthdefects.org

Email: staff@birthdefects.org

Phone: 407-895-0802

DR. TERITA F. GUSBY

OASIS MAAP Services for Autism, Asperger Syndrome & PDD

950 S. Court

St. Crown Point

IN 46307

MAAP Services for Autism and Asperger Syndrome and PDD is a nonprofit organization which provides networking, referrals, printed information for families and others who are involved in or concerned with individuals on the autism spectrum. MAAP was founded in 1984 and its mission is to ensure that all people with autism spectrum disorders have the proper ability to grow, learn and enjoy the best quality of life possible.

Web: http://www.aspergersyndrome.org

Email: info@aspergersyndrome.org

Phone: (219) 662-1311 (Mon-Thurs 9 AM to 3 PM CST)

DR. TERITA F. GUSBY

Center for Parent Information and Resources (formerly NICHCY)

35 Halsey St.

Fourth Floor

Newark, NJ 07102

The Center for Parent Information and Resources (formerly National Dissemination Center for Children with Disabilities [NICHCY]) website provides information to parents, teachers and communities. The general public can look up a specific disability and learn what each disability is and how to help with awareness in their community. The website also offers links to state agencies and parent groups all around the country. Making an early diagnosis and early intervention is the key to providing a better quality of life for all involved. The website offers free publications in both English and Spanish.

DR. TERITA F. GUSBY

Web: http://www.parentcenterhub.org

Email: malizo@spannj.org

Marcus Autism Center

Medical Clinic North Druid Hills, Georgia

National Institute of Child Health and Human Development (NICHD)

31 Center Drive

Building 31 Room 2A32

Bethesda

MD 20892-2425

NICHD was founded by President John F. Kennedy in 1962. The Institute was designed to study "the complex process of human development from conception to old age". NICHD supports human growth and development from conception to death. Research focuses on the developmental phases and functions of human life. This research includes developing therapies and intervention programs for all individuals with disabilities including autism.

Web: https://www.nichd.nih.gov

Email: NICHDInformationResourceCenter@mail.nih.gov

Phone: 1-800-370-2943

National Institute on Deafness & Other Communication Disorders

Information Clearing House (NIDCD)

31 Center Drive

Bethesda

MD 20892-2320

The National Institute on Deafness and Other Communication Disorders (NIDCD) conducts research in the processes of hearing, taste, balance, voice, smell language and speech.

Over 30% of children with autism never learn to speak using complete sentences. NIDCD began research in November of 2014 at Boston University to find out how hearing and speech affect or are affected by autism. This research program is called Unlocking Emily's World and is still in progress.

Web: http://www.nidcd.nih.gov

Email: nidcdinfo@nidcd.nih.gov

Phone: 800-241-1044

National Institute of Mental Health (NIMH)

6001 Executive Boulevard

Room 6200

Bethesda

MD 20892-9663

The National Institute of Mental Health provides basic, clinical research which will pave the way for prevention, recovery and ultimately a cure for mental health disorders including autism. The National Institute provides a vital and innovative role in public health, always striving for a breakthrough using novel methods to discover the science of the brain.

Web: http://www.nimh.nih.gov

Email: nimhinfo@nih.gov

Phone: 1-301-443-4279

Center for Autism and Related Disorders

Phone: 469-694-1754

818-758-8015

Email: infor@centerforautism.com

The Asperger / Autism Network (AANE)

85 Main Street, Suite 3

Watertown. MA 02472

American Academy of Pediatrics (AAP): Autism Initiatives

The AAP Autism Initiatives includes policy statements and clinical reports, information on autism prevalence, tools and resources for pediatricians, and resources for families.

The Arc

This agency promotes and protects the human rights of people with intellectual and developmental disabilities through policy and advocacy, initiatives on various aspects of life, and resources.

AUCD Network Centers

AUCD supports and promotes a national network of federally funded university-based interdisciplinary programs. These centers include the *University Centers for Excellence in Developmental Disabilities Education, Research, and Service (UCEDD)*, *Leadership Education in Neurodevelopmental Disabilities (LEND) Programs*, and *Intellectual and Developmental Disabilities Research Centers (IDDRCs)*.

Autism Science Foundation

ASF strives to support autism research by providing research funding and by providing information to the general public through their Weekly Science Podcast, Day of Learning, and more.

Autism Society

Autism Society provides advocacy, education, referrals, support, and more at the national, state, and local level through their nationwide network of affiliates.

Autistic Self Advocacy Network (ASAN)

ASAN seeks to advance the rights of people with autism. They are run by and for autistic people.

Autistic Women & Nonbinary Network (AWN)

AWN provides community, support, and resources for autistic women, girls, nonbinary people, and all others of marginalized genders.

Brain and Behavior Research Foundation

BBRF has awarded more than $11 million to autism research since 1987. This section features the latest research discoveries, news and events, and more.

The Center for Advancing Policy on Employment for Youth (CAPE-Youth)

CAPE-Youth was established to help states improve employment outcomes for youth and young adults with disabilities. They also provide information and resources for policymakers and the disability community.

The Council on Children with Disabilities (COCWD) Autism Subcommittee

The American Academy of Pediatrics' COCWD Autism Subcommittee provides evidence-based guidance on caring for children and teens on the autism spectrum.

Color of Autism

The Color of Autism supports African American children with autism and their families. The organization works to provide culturally competent resources for early and accurate diagnosis and empower families to advocate for services.

Eagles Autism Foundation

The Eagles Autism Foundation supports autism research that can improve the lives of individuals and families affected by autism. Their annual fundraising event is the Eagles Autism Challenge.

The Els for Autism Foundation

The Els for Autism Foundation is committed to better understanding the aspirations of people with autism spectrum disorder and helping them to fulfill their potential to lead positive, productive, and rewarding lives, through the development and delivery of interventions, educational programs, training programs, and recreational programs, and independent living programs; global outreach; and raising awareness and promoting inclusion of people on the autism spectrum.

Grupo Salto

Grupo Salto is a support group for Latino families who have children with disabilities, especially autism. They work to provide culturally competent information and services to families.

Interdisciplinary Technical Assistance Center (ITAC) on Autism and Developmental Disabilities

ITAC, which is part of the Association of University Centers on Disabilities (AUCD), provides guidance to interdisciplinary training programs that teach professionals how to screen and diagnose autism as well as provide evidence-based interventions.

International Disability Alliance

The International Disability Alliance is made up of 14 global and regional organizations that represent people with disabilities. They advocate at United Nations for disability inclusion across the globe.

International Society for Autism Research (INSAR)

INSAR is a scientific and professional organization that strives to advance knowledge about autism through providing opportunities for collaboration, mentorship, and education.

Madison House Autism Foundation

Madison House works to find, develop, and promote solutions that allow adults on the autism spectrum to live independently, find employment, and connect to their community.

MITRE Neurodiverse Federal Workforce Initiative

MITRE is collaborating with federal, academic, and private industry partners to launch a Neurodiverse Federal Workforce Initiative to increase high-tech career opportunities within the federal government for individuals on the autism spectrum.

Nancy Lurie Marks Family Foundation

This foundation develops and provides grants to programs in research, clinical care, policy, advocacy, and education in order to advance the understanding of autism.

National Association of Councils on Developmental Disabilities

NACDD is the national association for the 56 Councils on Developmental Disabilities (DD Councils) across the United States and its territories. The DD Councils receive federal funding to support programs that promote self-determination, integration and inclusion for all people in the United States with developmental disabilities.

National Autism Association (NAA)

The NAA promotes safety and addresses urgent needs of the autism community through advocacy, education, awareness, research and tools.

Organization for Autism Research (OAR)

OAR's mission is to use research to address the daily concerns of self-advocates, parents, autism professionals, and caregivers.

Simons Foundation Autism Research Initiative (SFARI)

SFARI is a scientific initiative that works to improve the understanding, diagnosis, and treatment of autism spectrum disorders.

Southwest Autism Research and Resource Center (SARRC)

SARRC is dedicated to autism research, education, evidence-based treatment, and community outreach and inclusion.

Simons Foundation/SPARK for Autism

SPARK for Autism supports autism researchers and encourages people on the autism spectrum and their families to participate in autism studies. They also host a webinar series and write articles to educate stakeholders on issues related to autism, such as mental health, general wellness, brain development, and more.

United States International Council on Disabilities

The United States International Council on Disabilities' mission is to advance international disability rights and inclusive development in the U.S. and abroad. They work to build bridges between governments, disability and human rights communities, and the private sector.

DR. TERITA F. GUSBY

INTERNATIONAL AUTISM ORGANIZATIONS

Worldwide there are thousands of autism organizations offering information, resources, and services. While you should always consult a physician if you are concerned your child may have autism, you may also have an autism organization in your country that could provide additional support. Here are just a few global agencies around the world.

ALBANIA

Albanian Children Foundation
Rr. "Deshmoret e 4 Shkurtit"
Pallati nr. 30
pas Carlsberg restorant
Tirana, Albania
P.O.Box 8285
Tel/Fax: + 35542270663;
Mob: + 355686027771
E-mail: coordinator@albanianchildren.org

ALGERIA

Ministere de la Sante et de la Population
17 Rue Abderahmane Laala
Algiers
Algeria

Phone: 213-261-5315

Fax: 213-265-3646

NIDAA Association of Autistic Children

Republic Avenue Merouana

Postal Code: 05300

Wilaya de Batna

Algeria

Phone: 00213773213099

Email: tamino70tr@yahoo.fr

ARGENTINA

APNA (Fundacion) Centro de rehabilitacion de jovenes autistas

Mendoza e Independencia 1623

3972 Ing. Maschwitz

Argentina

Phone: (540488417) 616-1830

Asociacion de Amigos del Nino Aislado (ADANA)

Marin Cornejo 9

4400 Salta

Argentina

Phone: 54 8731-3060

DR. TERITA F. GUSBY

Fax: 54 8739-4221

Email: aleherz@arnet.com.ar

AUSTRALIA

Asperger's Syndrome Support Network (Qld) Inc.

PO Box 159

Virginia Queensland 4014

Australia

Phone: 61-07-3865-2911

Fax: 61-07-3865-2838

Email: office@asperger.asn.au

Autism Behavioural Intervention NSW

Suite 202/35 Doody Street

Alexandria, NSW 2015

Australia

Phone: (02) 9669 2250

Fax: (02) 9669 2240

Email: info@abinsw.org.au

Autistic Citizens Residential & Resources Society of Victoria Inc.

P.O. Box 3015

Ripponlea, Victoria

Australia

Phone: 61-04-1738-4454

Email: dcoates@asd.org.au

AUSTRIA

Osterreichische Autistenhilfe

Esselingasse 13/3/11

A-1010 Wien

Vienna

Austria

Phone: 43-1-533-9666

Fax: 43-1-533-7847

Email: office@autistenhilfe.at

BANGLADESH

Autistic Children's Welfare Foundation, Bangladesh

House #74, Line #3, Block E

Kalshi, Mirpur-12

Dhaka-1216

Bangladesh

Telephone: 880-02-8019838 / 01914403331/4

Email: acwfbddhaka@gmail.com

Society for the Welfare of Autistic Children (SWAC)

70/KA, Pisciculture, Shyamoli,

Dhaka-1207

Bangladesh

Phone: 88 02 8118836, Mobile: 88 01711632861

Email: info@autism-swac.org OR mofijul@autism-swac.org

BERMUDA

Tomorrow's Voices – Bermuda Autism Early Intervention Centre

Registered Charity #816

155 South Road, Smith's HS 01

Bermuda

Tel: (441) 297-4342

Fax: (441) 297-2342

Email: tomorrowsvoices@northrock.bm

BOTSWANA

CamphillCommunity Rankoromane Trust
Camphill Rankoromane School
PO Box 2224
Gaborone
Botswana
Phone: 267-323-038
Email: camphill.friends@iname.com

BRAZIL
Associacao Brasileira de Autismo (ABRA)
Rua do Lavapes, 1123
Cambuci 0159-000
Sao Paulo
Brazil
Phone; 55-11-33764400

BRUNEI DARUSSALAM
Learning Ladders Society
Bungalow C11,
Spg 373-69,
Maktab Duli,

Gadong

Brunei Darussalam

Phone: +673 2457197

Email: learningladderssociety@gmail.com

Fax: 33-11-33764403

Email: falecomaama@ama.org.br

CANADA

AUTISM CANADA

P.O. Box 366

Bothwell, ON, N0P 1C0

Canada

Telephone: (519) 695-5858

Fax: (519) 695-5757

Email: info@autismcanada.org

Website: http://www.autismcanada.

Canadian National Autism Foundation

1227 Barton Street East

P.O. Box 47577

Hamilton, Ontario, L8H 2V0

Canada

Phone: 905-643-7183

Fax: 905-643-0969

Email: info@cnaf.net

QuebecFederation quebecoise de l'autisme et des autres troubles envahissants du developpement

65 rue de Castelnau Ouest, local 104

Montreal (Quebec) H2R 2W3

Canada

Phone: (514) 270-7386

Fax: (514) 270-9261

Email: secretariatfqa@contact.net

Autism Working Group Yukon

508 F Main Street

Whitehorse, Yukon Canada

Y1A 2B9

Phone: 867-667-6406

Fax: 867-667-6408

Email: info@autismyukon.org

INSAR

International Society for Autism Research

400 Admiral Blvd. Kansas City, Mo. 64106

DR. TERITA F. GUSBY

Email: info@autism-insar.org

The International Society for Autism Research (INSAR) is a scientific and professional organization devoted to advancing knowledge about autism. INSAR was formed in 2001 and is governed by an elected, volunteer Board of Directors who oversee all functions of the Society. Various committees assist the Board in carrying out the mission of the Society.

AUTISM CONNECT

ICAN International Conference for Neurodevelopmental disorders

India

References

The LEAP Outreach Project The Center for Collaborative Educational Leadership University of Colorado at Denver 1380 Lawrence Street Suite 650 Denver, CO 80204

Mandell, D. S., Morales, K. H., Xie, M., Lawer, L. J., Stahmer, A. C., & Marcus, S. C. (2010). Age of diagnosis among medicaid-enrolled children with autism, 2001–2004. *Psychiatric Service, 61*, 822–829.

Broder-Fingert, S., Feinberg, E., & Silverstein, M. (2018). Improving screening for autism spectrum disorder: Is it time for something new. *Pediatrics, 141*, e20180965.

Joyce, C., Honey, E., Leekam, S. R., Barrett, S. L., & Rodgers, J. (2017). Anxiety, intolerance of uncertainty and restricted and repetitive behaviour: Insights directly from young people with ASD. Journal of Autism and Developmental Disorders, 47(12), 3789-3802. https://doi.org/gk9z47

ALLY Pediatric Therapy

American Academy of Pediatrics

Child Mind Institute /Department of Neurosciences, UC San Diego 9500 Gilman Dr. La Jolla CA 92093

Ages & Stages Questionnaires®, Third Edition (ASQ-3™), Squires & Bricker E101360100 © 2009 Paul H. Brookes Publishing Co.

The Child Mind Institute Family Resource Center was made possible by a generous grant from the Morgan Stanley Foundation.

The International Board of Credentialing and Continuing Education Standards / US Office 4651 Salisbury Rd. Ste 340 Jacksonville, FL 32256: Dubai Office, Office 404, Al Saaha Offices-B. Souk Al Bahar, **Burj Kalifa District, PO Box 487177. Dubai-UAE**

Organization for Autism Research (OAR) www.researchautism.org 2000 N. 14th Street, Suite 710 Arlington, VA 22201 1-866-366-9710

Travel

Integrated Pediatric Therapies at 847.412.4379 or email ipi@jcfs.org

Call 855.ASK.JCFS (855.275.5237), email ask@jcfs.org or visit us online at jcfs.org

Francus, M. S. (n.d.). 7 Tips for Flying with an Autistic Child. MiniTime. Retrieved Jan.14,2024, from minitime.com/trip-tips/7-Tips-for-Flying-with-an-Autistic-Child-article

Goehner, A. L. (2009). Six Tips for Traveling with an Autistic Child. Time Magazine. Retrieved Jan.14, 2024, from content.time.com/time/specials/packages/article/0,28804,1893554_1893556_189

3538, 00.html

Schlosser, A. (n.d.). Ten Strategies for Traveling with a Child with Autism. Autism

Speaks. Retrieved Jan.14,2024
autismspeaks.org/sites/default/files/documents/family services/

schlosser.pdf

Linda Wilkins / Barriers to be Aware of as an Autistic Traveler

World Nomads Contributor - Tue, 16 Nov 2021

Come Fly with Me: Travel Tips for Children with Autism Spectrum Disorder
by Eliana Wool, M.A., Psychological Services Pre-Doctoral Intern

CDC-Source: National Center on Birth Defects and Developmental Disabilities, Centers for Disease Control and Prevention

1. Lord C, Risi S, DiLavore PS, Shulman C, Thurm A, Pickles A. Autism from 2 to 9 years of age. Arch Gen Psychiatry. 2006 Jun;63(6):694-701.
2. Hyman SL, Levey SE, Myers SM, Council on Children with Disabilities, Section on Developmental and Behavioral Pediatrics. Identification, Evaluation, and Management of Children with Autism Spectrum Disorder. Pediatrics. 2020 Jan;145(1).

Asperger's Syndrome - Nationwide Children's Hospital NationwidE Children's Hospital. https://www.nationwidechildrens.org

Administration for Community Living (2020). Rehabilitation Act. Retrieved from Rehabilitation

Act | ACL Administration for Community Living

Braddock, D. L., (2017). The State of The States in Intellectual and Developmental Disabilities:

2017 [Presentation] Long Beach California. http://stateofthestates.org

"Caretaker." Merriam-Webster.com Dictionary, Merriam-Webster, https://www.merriam-

webster.com/dictionary/caretaker.

Centers for Medicare & Medicaid Services. Home & Community-Based Services 1915(c).

Retrieved from Home & Community-Based Services 1915(c) | Medicaid

Coyle, C. E., Kramer, J., Mutchler, J. E. (2014). Aging together: Sibling carers of adults with

intellectual and developmental disabilities. Journal of Policy and Practice in Intellectual

Disabilities, 11(4), 302-312. doi: 10.1111/jppi.12094

Kim, S., Larson S. A., Lakin, K. C. (2001) Behavioral outcomes of deinstitutionalization for

people with intellectual disability: A review of US studies conducted between 1980-1999.

Journal of Intellectual and Developmental Disability, 26(1), 35-50.

https://doi.org/10.1080/13668250020032750

Lee, C., & Burke, M. M. (2020). Future planning among families of individuals with intellectual

and developmental disabilities: A systematic review. Journal of Policy and Practice in

Intellectual Disabilities, 17(2), 94-107. doi: 10.1111/jppi.12324

Meldon, P. (2017). Disability history: Early and shifting attitudes of treatment. Retrieved from

Telling All Americans' Stories (U.S. National Park Service) (nps.gov)

Smith DaWalt, L., Hong, J., Mailick M. R., Greenberg, J. S. (2019). Mortality in individuals with autism spectrum disorder: Predictors over a 20-year period. Autism, 23(7), 1732-1739.

https://doi.org/10.1177/1362361319827412

U.S. Department of Health & Human Services (2023). Housing. Retrieved from Housing

Resources for Autism - Websites and Program | IACC (hhs.gov)

U.S. Department of Housing and Urban Development (2023). Physical Accessibility. Physical

Accessibility | HUD.gov / U.S. Department of Housing and Urban Development (HUD)

Williamson, H. J., Perkins, E. A., Massey, O. T., Bladwin, J. A., Lulinski, A., Armstrong, M. I., &amp.

Levins, B. L. (2018) Family caregivers as needed partners: Recognizing their role in. Medicaid manages long-term services and supports. Journal of Policy and Practice in Intellectual Disabilities, 15(3), 214-225.

Diagnosis

1. Lord C, Risi S, DiLavore PS, Shulman C, Thurm A, Pickles A. Autism from 2 to 9 years of age. Arch Gen Psychiatry. 2006 Jun;63(6):694-701.

2. Hyman SL, Levey SE, Myers SM, Council on Children with Disabilities, Section on Developmental and Behavioral Pediatrics. Identification, Evaluation, and Management of Children With Autism Spectrum Disorder. Pediatrics. 2020 Jan;145(1).

Drug Use

Aman, M. G., McDougle, C. J., Scahill, L., Handen, B., Arnold, L. E., Johnson, C., et al.; the Research Units on Pediatric Psychopharmacology Autism Network. (2009). Medication and parent training in children with pervasive developmental disorders and serious behavior problems: Results from a randomized clinical trial. *Journal of the American Academy of Child & Adolescent Psychiatry, 48*(12), 1143-1154.

Be Aware of Potentially Dangerous Products and Therapies that Claim to Treat Autism. (n/d). Retrieved May 28, 2019, from https://www.fda.gov/consumers/consumer-updates/be-aware-potentially-dangerous-products-and-therapies-claim-treat-autism

Potenza, M., & McDougle, C. (1997). New findings on the causes and treatment of autism. *CNS Spectrums, Medical Broadcast Limited.*

<u>Treatments</u>

National Institute of Mental Health. (2011). A parent's guide to autism spectrum disorder. Retrieved March 8, 2012, from http://www.nimh.nih.gov/health/publications/a-parents-guide-to-autism-spectrum-disorder/index.shtml

Kotte, A., Joshi, G., Fried, R., Uchida, M., Spencer, A., Woodworth, K. Y., et al. (2013). Autistic traits in children with and without ADHD. *Pediatrics, 132*(3), e612–e622.

PRESCRIPTIONS / (843) 369-0600 (office)

Website—

https://www.educationprescriptions@gmail.com /

DR. TERITA F. GUSBY

Made in the USA
Columbia, SC
17 March 2025